THESE BLANK PAGES ARE FOR YOU, THE READERS!

Write like it's a journal if you like…Write down what comes to you when you read this Beautiful book of poetry written by Dana S. Bicks. I hope that you enjoy them and find the needed love and comfort in these poems and hope that you find whatever you are looking for…Enjoy! And may God Bless You All, Always….

My Deepest Appreciation and Dedication

Before I list all those who have given of themselves countless hours, thoughts and ideas; may I first and foremost say thanks be to God. I thank God for this gift, to be able to write and, by which all of my poetry is "heaven sent." I can assure you, growing up dyslexic - writing was not on my priority list.

But, "May God bless, Janice, who suffered countless hours of relentless organizing, as she in the process with helping me; Sharon Byrd who saw my creativity, and connected me with Lisa Marie, her friend who has mentored and guided me through the course of my direction.

I want to think Jessie for helping get the cover going and helping Lisa and Jan through trying to publish my book. Thank you Katie for fixing the cover...Thank you Raven Publishing for doing all the media and pages you created to market this book.. It's a dream come true.

But most of all, God brought me the most wonderful understudy, and one who I could ever artistically had written about! A lady of dignity and grace; a role model to her gender - where class and poise dominates; a widow before her time, and now three generations of love and support to carry her on. Anonymously - has inspired and honored and, God has blessed me with the ability to write about a love not many could imagine.

And, "By God's Grace," I did - just that! As life goes on, I'll sculpture in poetry!

Preface

Breach and blue, I came into this world. My parents divorced when I was five, and my father passed when I was thirteen....a "middle" child I learned later – I wasn't retarded, I was dyslexic. School was unbearable but, I struggled to pass. Married early! It was the thing to do during the Viet Nam era. "Make love not war," seemed to be a way life in those changing times, I grew up in...

I was good with my hands and learned to build and now from a broken family Life was unstable at best. I was fairly creative – however designing, building, and remodeling as well. My roots could not have been from a better place to grow up outside Annapolis.

Yet as unstable as life sometimes can be, we find our roots take us home to where our life started. "By God's Grace," somehow… we all make it! Today as I sit, I look back to '09 when I picked up a pen and began to write. Like a wild stallion, I was loose, and with no direction; but, now I see poetically that my life has unfolded into the pages before you. I pray you open your heart as you read, and may I touch you with what I wrote. A lefty all my life, God and His divine humor thought He'd make me right handed when I write my poetry! May God be with you!!!...

12 Degrees

As we all sit and wait on spring, I think, "it's late," At 12 degrees and freezing cold - there's very little warmth outside in the fallen snow. But even at 12 degrees, as there's very little heat -nonetheless - there is some! Yes, I feel the warmth - even at 12 degrees. It's a heat wave that's generated from above that comforts me; and, the snow covers like a blanket to protect those spring bulbs warming from the dead of cold in the persistent winter...

In the bitter cloud covered cold, the flurries of joy bring welcome relief; and, a shroud of heat as I smile with optimism for tomorrow, the sun returns! Happiness brings warmth - you know; Spring, brings forth joy, and the Lord above orchestrates with his love - even at 12 degrees. His ever presence prevails, for faith in the future, holds. The frozen roads and the icy windows will be long gone when the sun's warmth finally returns...

Yes! Even in those 12 little degrees, I feel the warmth through the clouds of the setting sun; the cold and snow is temporary, but the love in my heart; the joy in my soul, burns like an eternal flame as it generates warmth from its somber glow.
And there as in a relay, the torch is passed for our Lord carries the burden of the cold as we all pray for the warmth of Spring. Our 12 degrees, "yes" it's chilly - but we hold our faith against the cold and brave the penetration from the wind.

So Lord, we look to you to keep the warmth and happiness in our hearts and souls - as we are out; and, weather the storm in that not so balmy 12 degrees of warmth.....

A Blessing From Above

    I sat on the shore and listened to the waves as each one had its own distinctive sound; my toes half buried in the sand - I thought about my past; and, wished for so much more! Mentally, I measured the distance between the breaks; the waves gave a rhythm too old… Mother Earth, keeping constant time like the sun as it approached. A hand tapped me on the shoulder; "Let's go for a walk!" "Why not," I said. You reached out to me and took my hand. You could tell I was deep in thought over something.

As we enjoyed the quietness, we walked along the ocean's edge. "What's wrong?" you asked….you seemed so distant. "Oh my dear" "You're too kind!" "Your observance is much appreciated; but it's nothing to do with you at all! I just caught myself looking back where life had made some really wrong turns; and, asking "Why in the world, do the paths we follow really lead us where there's no tomorrow?"

As you held my hand; your touch; oh…..the comfort I felt from you in the morning sun! You splashed me with your toes as you kicked the salt right out of the water; playfully frolicking in the shallows. Your youth is overwhelming as you run off down beach. "Catch me if you can!!" "Oh, you knew what you were doing!!!" The joyful love you gave to me, spread across the horizons of the oceans. I finally figured that God had a hand in this, somehow.

I watched your vibrancy as you spelled out "I love you – Dana," in the sand. This is what my heart had always wanted for so, "so" many years; but then, that thought brought me back to where I was before you touched me on the shoulder... sitting on the sand with thoughts of growing old. We must endure the pain before the pleasure! I looked out as a school of dolphin caught my attention. We stopped and held hands to give reverence to them as they blessed us in the morning light, as if a sign from God… "Just hold on! "Everything was going to be alright!" We turned to continue on our merry way, tickling each other as we laughed in the morning sun.

As the sun began to warm us through our clothes; the "joy" of us holding hands, and walking in the shallow waters. I thought to myself, only God could bring this gift for only he knew what I'd been through. The sunsets are all numbered; and, the cool evening breezes have reached us up here to refresh our tired and weary bodies. Let us lay here by this open window, and share in the luster of holding hands and making love as we walk along the ocean's edge --- captivated by one another.

I LOVE YOU FOREVER…..

A Day to Remember

I ran the kids off to school, and headed off to work. It was a pretty day as I remembered as early sign of color in the trees, gave a luster to the oncoming season. After work, I mowed the yard; the kids played hockey stick out in the street, as the sun set across the lake. Sitting on the porch having a glass of wine, I thanked God for the world was round, and everything seemed to be according to scripture. I helped put the young ones to bed; sat, and chatted with my wife for a minute; toasted to the refreshing breeze as it filtered up the creek from the open waters. I got in bed and looked to the heavens, and thought, "Thank you Jesus for a wonderful day," and closed my eyes; slowly drifted off to a peaceful night of sleep.

The morning came and I was up before the chickens, taking care of breakfast and making sandwiches for the kids. Another - you know - normal day; my wife went off to the office; the big kids caught the bus; and, my sweet Melissa needed to be dropped off at kindergarten. With my chores complete, back to the house to catch a little news before I started my day.

I turned on the tube to see the first tower, up in flames; called my brother; "Oh my God!" … "Brother, what the hell is happening? As he spoke, "we are under attack"; the second one caught another airplane. Almost in slow motion, I thought I was watching an action movie…"Did the TV switch channels by itself?"
There "under God," our way of life now under attack; our lives would be for ever changed; for those who believe in being undivided, "its-too-late; our country - now broken; our system off center; and, as the morning comes…

 I pray, "Lord, let us be granted with the security, and faith that…maybe, our homeland will stand under the promises of our forefathers; and as the sun sets on the Pacific anointing the night, let the heavenly angels guard our nation! Amen.

A Night with You

   Picture this! Headed east; a gentle breeze; you and me; that's all we need! Ok, maybe three - and the Good Lord too! "Nope!" I'm wrong! Now it's four: the moon as orange as any you've ever seen has made an appearance through the trees. In the night fall air, so crisp and surreal; a breath taking view to enjoy - perfectly made for me and you!

   The sails gleam as the moon reflects its glow. You are beside me, snuggled - sharing the warmth that flows between us. The only noise we hear is the water rippling along as our little yacht sails off - into the harvest moon!

   As God has kissed the breeze; you turn to me, and kiss my cheek. I ask, "What was that for?" You gently back away – smiling; and, you say "It's been a long time since I drifted away! "The ambience has captured me!" "My heart has come to another shore!" For to many years I too, have sailed across these waters and to no avail! I see now what God has done. He kissed the night - for us to be alone.

   O what a picture perfect moment; if I could only frame this second where God has shown a way for us to sail off to the heavens! Now the moon up high gives a luster to the lake below. Quietly, we sail along listening; smiling! There's nothing wrong.

   "Oh look!" - A shooting star has left its mark as it races across the mid-night sky; and, there you are, lying in my arms - your back up against me. The air has cooled a degree or two. The blanket we brought along, firmly wrapped around your knees; telling me, "It's time to go home!"

   If it's only for the moment that we come out here and share; for this is a gift from God. The origin of life; that we sail away to our destiny - where dreams are made; and, memories are too - of you!

A Quarter Moon

I sat alone today, my coffee and me; and, watched the sky for it anointed "thy." The sun shone through the weathered leaves; it was a Friday, I believe. I can't remember now!

The sun is gone and all alone – it's just me and my quarter moon. "Oh, it's so white, and bright; you'd think it was full!" But it was not, a quarter or two was all it was. Poised as fall ushers in; the rain will soon begin; but for now, the sky is blue, and I sit here under this quarter moon.

I thought about going out to my favorite place; but, sat and thought "not," for I too, could just sit here, and enjoy the quarter moon. The night is young - younger than me; but, the moon is smiling down for us all to see; the glory that has come over me, as its bright light seizes the darkness; the light of summers almost gone, reminds me of the romance I once knew and now – it's gone; but, it's okay - for me and the moon agree…that God will grant us another day!

I enjoy the gentle breeze that employs the moon to light the sky, as I sit and watch the night; God hath made "day" that I enjoyed; and, now the "night" before the winter brings.

Am I - I Am

Sitting in the dark- waiting; a message comes to me in tune, as I am. A candle burns, for God has posed a question to me; "What do I want to be - you see? " We all have a calling; and, I asked from God – "What are your goals?" – "How high are your sights?" As God speaks - I listen; for in the dark - He said, "Relax - for here I am!" "You must be patient!" My heart races… I feel the blood, and adrenaline charging through my system; my toes cold, my forehead itches, my nerves are on end; for what is it that The Lord has called on me to help him? - What could I, a poor sinner ever do - that would be what God could need of me? As I sit here alone – it's about 3:35 in the morn; a thought comes to me. "God, don't you sleep…for why am I awake? "Why is it you have beaconed me?" I am old, and I am tired…for what is my calling? What is your desire? I should have put socks on - my toes are so cold. I try to sit with my feet under me; but, they won't - too old!"

I listen as my left hand writes -it's November 8, 2013. Is it significant, or should it be? I don't know…its 37 degrees outside! It feels the same in here to me, though I wish that candle would warm my feet!

My love is asleep…. I think or I hope…I wouldn't know. She's not here - you know; just me and Jesus My Lord, to whom I pray for blessings…for this year to be different for me, than all the years before. He hears!!! I know….but still - I wait in the dark; in the cold, for I pick up my pen, a message to relay. I sit ready; shorthand maybe, to write the message for which I intend to have discerned on me. I pray, "Lord, what might it be that I can help you? - I'm not worthy to be in your room. Yet you're here, standing beside me. I'm in awe! What should I do? - My feet are freezing; my heart is warm, a message from an angel-lady; a friend I knew, way back when, "Florence" was her name. I don't understand the significance. Why did she email me at 3:54 in the morn? – "Lord it's you!" "I wait to receive your sacraments."

Oh lord my heart goes out to another -I adore. The love of my life, to marry; maybe - be my wife! Be blessed by you, but presents/prevails here in this room. I rub my face, a chill there too. I know you're here! - I have felt your presence before in a hotel in Carolina some months ago. "Lord," I ask. "What is it that you call upon me to help you with?" "Shall I be alert, and observe - my attention on your demand?" "Yes Lord! - I am your servant…to serve!" "How can I lend you a hand?" "What is it you have bestowed on me?" I listen!!! - Rejoice comes after Reaction…….

Autumn Shadows

As I went for my first crisp evening walk, the cool and dampened chill refreshed my spirit as the full moon held me captive in the night air. Tonight the moon smiled upon the earth; where the sun now gone away from a busy day, replaced by the love that only the glow could shed upon us.

The dim lit shadows in shades of dark gray accents the foliage that lines the way. For they say the entrance to heaven - a resilient white light maybe; or, it's not - but rather, a cool peaceful quiet; and, shadows upon the ground from the full of moonlight as the branches pay homage to the autumn day. A night owl stands guard announcing your coming, I wonder!…

Yes, as we walk through the valleys, some may even reside. But, let not your heart have an ounce of despair as the moon casts its heavenly rays upon you. As you climb in and recite prayers, you close your eyes; and, travel another land…..there in disbelief, you lie wondering.... But oh 'ye' of little faith! And, "Where in this world can you find - Moon dust?" ....

As you first rub, does not the grit and sand left in the very ducts as water flows… as dust being left in your hands as you wipe it from your sleepy eyes? When morning comes; "Yes!" It's there in the autumn shadows we walk; giving thanks to God for I know our roads aren't paved with gold; but, the thoughts of fall are worth a million bucks!....

Behind the Blind

There I walk down an up-rooted old sidewalk, where maples have lifted, and broken the concrete. The autumn's leaves, peaked in color; and, a northern chill invites thoughts of winter. Careful not to trip on the uneven pieces of concrete; and. mesmerized by the architecture of an era gone by…the craftsmanship captivates my inspiration. I gander at the lace draped windows, and the shears that curtain the panes. Trying not to be obvious - the ripples in the handmade glass, reflect the afternoon rays that pragmatically glare at me, causing me to meditate a minute. "Oh, I think, the weather those windows have seen." And there showing between the first and second floor, a little wagon wheel ...

In my bomber jacket and a collegiate scarf, trying to stay warm - shedding the cold and leaning against the old maple trunk, I stand staring, wondering why in world would you ever place a blind on such an interesting piece of creativity.

But all alone, this little window, meant to light the stairway showing the way contained a blind, blocking out the daylight. "Why!" I wonder? "Why would you want to hide in your life - in the stairwell of all things?" Almost to commemorate that wagon wheel window, I stood in reverent silence.

The blind blocked the very purpose of its duty, protecting you as you climb day to day through life - almost. I thought how it resembled the way some live, I guess; not allowing God to come into their life to light their path to walk; not to mention, the broken concrete beneath my feet which had crumbled over time....

Pondering, "What if there were no handrails to hold?" "Hmmmm," --- Then the front door opened, I watched an arm, an old flannel plead sweater - a rickety old cane - kicking a black cat out on to the weathered paint stained porch. I shook my head and thought some more.....

I couldn't take it! I walked up the broken steps, greeted by the black flee lion just wanting to be pet. I peeked through the webs and discolored shears; and there with his back to me, was white hair hunched in an old rocking chair. The cane was gone, and cardboard took its place with an afghan draped over his knees; he sat and rocked, watching his black and white.

For life had stopped living just waiting on the end; sitting in the dark, forgotten by many - a decrepit old man's only friend was the black cat he just kicked out the door. Quietly, I stepped away and retreated to street below. I pet the cat in sympathy, and stumbled on what's left of the steps, pulling up my collar, walking away....

Today, I look back and wonder how the old man's doing; or, if he's even alive; but most of all I wonder why he shut God out, even the black cat didn't stand a chance! But there, behind the blinds, lived a hell of man that loved his wife more than life itself; and, waited on God to take him home, where happiness and joy reside. And me -- I just stand watching a little of his final chapter....

Breaking Bread

It was early in the morn, I smelt the ingredients while walking to the kitchen. Entombed on the counter; the loaves of bread, the beginning of the season was upon us. It's time to give thanks to all those who had made this year a little easier for us.

The shorts and t-shirts had turned to football, and wrapping gifts. The trees have lost their summer foliage; and, the wet black bark stands somberly against the shades of gray; the ambers still aglow from night before. The house has turned into a winter wonderland of sorts.

Getting our day under way, a prayer…our coffee in bed with the morning news - watching the weather; rain may change to snow. Later, with an apron on; I watch you scurry around the kitchen. The family will all be here on Thursday! Getting ready to share the season; it is your favorite time of year!

The bread has risen; moist, golden brown, perfect for a holiday tradition. I sat and watched you, unaware - focused on perfection; cradled the loaves to an empty shelf, closed the door to the refrigerator; and, to your right, smiling at you stood, "Jesus in your kitchen." Gasping in His glory, you turned to the counter reaching for the last loaf, and handed it to Him. Like looking down from heavens and watching, you pulled out the chair - He smiled and reclined. He gestured to you to do the same; together, you and He - broke bread. I too smiled for only God could make this happen; a communion of two how blessed.

Never issuing a word; Jesus came calling on this dreary day; the brightest of bright; and, shined on your table - the sacrament of life beside you. As He came; so He left, but… a broken twig lay on the table where you had broken bread. I watched the tears stream as you took a napkin and wiped your cheek; in heaven smiling, He hath made a place watching you; preparing….there too, your day will come…….

Breathless

I sat here in the corner as the gentle, soon to be stormy breeze comforted me. I thought about last night, as I tried to replay the feelings we cast to one another; and in the last of the summer heat; I felt a "gift" from God! I smiled and touched the miracle that held me, for where dreams come from; prayers are answered!

Recollecting lying on the lawn where the stars blanket us with love, there in the autumn air; I felt your warmth. We watched to see the heavens move reverently, yet they did not; but, rather kept us in its grip. Suspiciously watching the stars as they twinkled in the night, I held you! .....

As I stole a kiss from you; you wrapped your arms around my neck; and, under that giant sky, we fell in love! And as we gave like right on cue; a shooting star commandeered the night. We looked, watched, and felt the unearthly power as though God had hit a grand slam - right out of the park!

Almost as though God had blessed our sanctuary in the back yard with fireworks from the heavens; we watched, all bundled up and trying to keep warm. All I could do was 'Thank' Our Lord for the blessing - He bestowed. Tomorrow shall be here in a couple hours; the stars will rest; and, we will rise again to be with our Lord; and there it is "only God," who can dictate what the future holds!

 I pray for your contentment; and, as the sun sets again tomorrow, may the heavens welcome the day that's past! .... Amen!

Bus Ride

Buying a ticket is the easiest part of any trip. As you climb on board, you store your things, looking for your seat. I wonder, "Who will sit beside me? "Who's across the aisle?" I wonder where they're off to. I pray - I will be safe. So I take my seat, believing the driver knows where he's going. Do we? We wonder if we'll meet someone that would be nice to talk to.... Never dreaming of life changing circumstances.....

But in the early morn, we board to destinies unknown. God never said that life was going to be easy - all the time; but, have faith, and pray; enjoy the ride. As you take your seat, you pray for God's mercy. You feel the bus in reverse...There - half awake, the bus bounces and sways as it leaves; the terminal now a distant past. Your life is now in another's hands. "Oh, it's a good time to say a prayer."

Across the aisle, a "Good morning!" gets exchanged! "Morning to you," reserved by race as life is now, contained in the place that you remain - sitting at all times. Generic conversation starts. We see our comforts are all but lost - left back where getting on was getting off. A nerve that touches the heart; and, dialog deserves to have a response as the countryside passes by your window. A stop or two to stretch your legs; potty breaks, and wash your face. We filter back into the place where life has commanded us to stand; sitting in our seat… or is it a pew; where we pray that God protects us. For now, dialog has turned to deep conversation. Some exchange seats, and some move in to hear. How two lives that just met, are so deeply intertwined; and, there's not a shade of difference as interpretation settles deep in your mind.

Yes, for some - God has found a seat in the bus ride. To where, we are not sure. Where are we going? He is there --- riding along --- listening as two lives have intermingled; and, though thoughts - now three years ago are so close. Siblings have grown too - to know how close we became riding along sharing a ride to destinations unknown... So as life rides, and carries you along where faith may be your only friend; never let the fellowship be divided by aisle; for across the way, there is always someone reaching out - maybe to help or just to pray. But remember the bumps and, as the bus sways. God is there; listening, as miracles are made - in Gods timing.

Castles in the Sand

    One of my most favorite things to do every summer, when we vacation at the shore; is to build a castle in the sand; and, watch the water run through the tunnels. I build a mote to trap the water, and float my boat in the pond around the castle water.

Mom lets me use a kitchen knife to carve the windows and doors as I pretend the people in the castle have to see out, and leave to get out and go about. Their speed boat waits in the little pond to take them for a ride; and - off they go - out from underneath the tunnel, to their private pond to play, and fish - enjoy the sun. "That is," Until a big ocean wave comes and washes it all away!

 Oh well! I build a new castle than before and better then the last one, with water falls and gardens; a place to sit and watch the waves. It would be so nice to have a friend like you, to play with on the beach with me, and build a world where we could pretend that we live in our own little ---our Castle in the Sand!

Charred Remains

Meandering up, I could still smell the charred remains of what was home. Standing on the blackened slab of what once was our garage; the tears began to flow as l looked across to the neighbor's yard. I stepped up where the kitchen was; kicking things - looking to see if anything was worth saving; but, all that stood now was starting to rust; refrigerator, not much more than memories - were left of us loving and cooking in the kitchen.

The dining room was much the same. Some wedding silver melted together from the intense heat; a piece of dining room table leg, and the metal claw foot lying on the ruined oriental. I looked to the right; the fireplace stood proudly, even though it was covered with soot. The big screen we used to cuddle with and watch; was only a testimony to a past life, we once had.

Panning through that which once was, I wandered through the charred two by fours, and walked into our memories of matrimony; and, somehow buried under our disintegrated mattress, lay our wedding album. I sat on the only un-charred corner, weeping again. I went through the torched ceremonial pages; and, on the last page totally unharmed - our invitation to celebrate 10/13/81.

I took the book and walked away, knowing there was nothing left of what we had worth saving. Exhausted with our way of life; the kids now grown; and, certainly nothing here to tie you down, our "to death do us part," --- came early. I knew this was what you wanted.

And there on a beautiful autumn day, instead of working in the yard, I'm forced to walk away, and do no less than ask our Lord, "Where do I turn to start over?" Tomorrow, I plan to stand where we shared vows and prayed. Somehow, He vindicates. For only He in his magnificent ways can save me from these "charred remains".

Chasing Rainbows

Today in the breezy blue sun rays; I watched as the fields of wheat whispered in the wind. I sat and thought of the days that might have been. I watched a rainbow appear out of nowhere; and, to my surprise - it was right there before me! Oh, I thought; "How I wish, I had someone beside me to see this miracle appear in front of me."

I stood to see if the end was near; maybe if I was lucky - a pile of gold would be within my reach. I started to walk to see if it landed somewhere out there in the field. But lo-n-behold; I heard the sounds of a little boy, and a little girl running across in front of me. I smiled again! It reminded me of me. They too were headed to that pot of gold. Over the hill and thru the field, I watched to see what their efforts would produce. I picked up my pace to catch a glimpse; but, the closer I got - the rainbow faded away, and the voices - they too became distant. I stopped!

"So, what was the point, I thought to myself." "Why?" "Was it even - ever there? But - the voices were real; or, at least - so I thought! And I ask…What was the point, Lord; to hear the breeze flowing through the wheat?" "No," He said, "I wanted you to see that I make the rainbows but gold - yet it may be in reach if you let your heart hold the key that opens the door." So, if your life has you chasing rainbows; and, you catch yourself looking for the gold. Behold – it just might be at the other end of the rainbow!!!

Christmas List

    It's that time again -for as it draws near; I think of things I need to do; but, this year will be different - because - now "there's you!" For years that passed, I sat - parades and football; a call to my brother…we wished "happy merry" to one another. This year - oh my! It will be such a delight…for I have you to share it with! "Happy- am I!"

    So my list, I want to share with you; now it's longer - a multiple of two - cause now there's you....I need to include. But as for me - my list was you! An early Christmas gift from God…for He knew it was "you," I prayed for. - On this Holiday, we share the gift of love. Our time we spend is new; from holding hands - to seeing our breath form a kiss that commands us to hug, and warms our hearts.

    Decorating the house with love; lights and ornaments…a wreath on the door; "Good cheer to all," the sign reads as you cross the threshold of the entry -for be blessed as you come in; stand by the fire, let me get you a cup of cheer to warm your heart; "Oh, what a wonderful time to fall in love!" – Ha; and they thought it was only Spring. What do they know; don't tell 'em a thing! It will be our secret for years to come.

    The shopping is done, the tree complete with gifts from Santa for the kids to share; and, treats on Christmas morn. "Oh, it'll be a time to remember as we, together - sit and watch as they smile, and give thanks!" "Breakfast is on the table; a wonderful day! "Look - a flurry!" "No, there's another!" Oh, that's great…God has blessed our day to cover it in winter white; delighted, we will enjoy our first snow together. A walk later after dinner; and, listening to the snow fall as it does from the heavens, there before our eyes. And, caroling from afar; wise man still search; but, you and me "We," have each other! A love so complete …to look any further would just be - a waste of time! Yes, it's our first of many to share, for the rest of our lives' for God has given us a second chance - to romance in the joy that holidays' bring.

    Yes, my Christmas list was short! There was just one thing on my list; though God knew what was on that list too!!! That's why - He brought me –"You!"

Closing Doors

I sat and watched as the crew came and covered the field. Lightning and thunder had moved in. The bleachers had emptied and heavy rain drops began to fall; yielding to the weather. I remained in the dugout and watched it pour. One of the kid's caps lie on the field, drenched. I thought how God had stopped the game; a summer time shower perhaps; and, as I sat inhaling the refreshing, cooled air; listening to the thunder get louder; I thought, up in the heavens, "God has slammed a door; a clap so loud it would make you come straight out of your chair; and then in the pouring rain, I asked, "Why do you decide it's time to close one, before you open another?" A little bit of blue sky showed through; and in a quiet voice, I heard "Yes; and, I'll wash the slate clean - if I want to -as well."

So I stood listening like a child from a scolding parent, with nothing more I could do in the pouring rain; but listen…and…walk away. I guess it was just for me to hear as the ball field was empty, my Lord scolding me. I smiled and under my breath; I chuckled! Who'd believe what has happened? Not even me! Could pretend I didn't hear it…. And --- As we so often get caught up in our routines and rituals, I find it curious why more of us don't take time to listen when in the thunder… who knows - it just might be our lord trying to communicate with us in the pouring down rain.

The next day came and practice resumed; the cracking of the bat reminded me of thunder. I watched and wondered of all places; why would our lord address me here in the pouring rain? I guess, "He knew; He certainly had my undivided attention!!!

Cuddling On the Couch

For once just for a day I wish I was artist! Oh, it's nice to write alright; but, I think to paint would be insane! I thought, "How cool it would be, to be Norman, and paint a couple of old folks cuddling on the couch." Maybe I should be the study, instead of the artist. I don't have the patience to paint you see; but, nonetheless, I think about a couple as they cuddle on the couch.

Running across the floor; a mouse! The old lab with his eyes closed, lying on the braided rug -his nose upon his toes; and granny can't see a thing, just knows she's by her old hubby by the smell of his old clothes. The cat, old and gray, lies on the arm of that old rickety couch; pops scratching his nape -watching as the mouse dares to ruin the portrait family shot.

Yes, I'd sit behind the easel. The colors would fly upon the sheet. I need to be as quick as I can - pops got diarrhea. The mouse has got his eyes on me; my feet would be high in the air as Max the lab, now zeroing in. The cat has changed position for attack is on command; but, pop sees the mouse. The cats not going anywhere! - Not with pops' hand grabbing at his nape.

Oh for a day to express, a moment in time that even "Kodak" can't capture. "How great I'd say - to be the one who catches pops and granny, sitting there."

Dancing With You

Sitting in the recliner, resting from another hot summer's day; I really have no desire to go anywhere; but thinking of you, I'm wishing you were here to rub my tired feet; then I remember our dinner date. I need to shower and make myself presentable. I always want to look as nice as I can "for you."

Coming to pick you up, I felt the love I own… it's all I have! "Yes it's grown; but it's the warmth we share, that has made our romance intensify. Yet tonight - dead tired, I promised you a romantic dinner with candle light and soft music; maybe even a dance or two! We got a table in a very quiet corner; where having a conversation, you decide to take your foot out of your sandal and rub my calf muscle; well, so much for my concentration! "Let's dance!" I thought it was safer than sitting across from you getting absconded; Lord knows what you were up to!

We chatted and danced to a few until, I guess, it was quarter-till twelve. The crowd had thinned. I thought it was finally our turn to leave as well. Driving home, you sat unusually close! I loved it, but it was abnormal for you! I knew you had an ulterior motive somewhere in the back of your mind. I could smell the smoke emerging from your brain. ..... You were up to no good! ....

I opened the door to a totally dark living room. I reached for the switch; you grabbed my arm and said, "Let me light a candle." "Ok, I said….that sounds even better. I turned the old hifi on, and found a 33; nothing but a little "Smokey" to fill the air in the living room. We sat on the couch, your head rested on my shoulder with my right arm, I held you tight as we reminisced about the old days, when we heard these songs for first. Temptations were waiting!!! Oh the days of plastic; my impulses were mounting. I kissed your neck behind your ear, and took my tongue; licked you gently as I kissed your tension from the day away...

And in middle of daylight and dawn, the stars sparkled; the heavens looked down; and, blessed the night. Slowly, one at a time, we started getting comfortable. The music mingled in our hearts as memories were embraced. Feelings between us sparkled brightly in the flickering candle light; and there in the middle of my living room floor we stood, hugging slowly --- dancing naked. .....

Dearly

Underneath a blanket where the heavens greet the earth, there's a place where we can touch the Love - we hold so "dearly." It's not in a home or a berth; on a boat; but, a place where we discover, that love is deeper than any void that was created by hurt if someone goes away. So sad, that God intervenes. Yet, its best you know - for only He can see the duration of the pain that remains after the love is demolished by divorce, or a death.

I cry and wonder; "What's the price of hurt?" "Do we deserve to have to pay the cost, just so we can move forward to a new love - we 'so much' want to create?" I guess, maybe; and, if God won't give us more than we can handle; then "Why? -Why are we so stubborn about letting go?"

I sit here in a quiet afternoon trying to depict, "Is love really worth the pain; for now I look, and watch those we know, that have been such a part of our lives, "Gone…Dads and moms - some siblings. We thought we'd go before them!

Oh, how I wish I knew God's plan. Yet there, as the thunder rolls in, surely there'll be rain. And - God will cleanse the earth; and, rid the world of imperfections as we again try to recover from the loss - where love has been.....

Dreaming of You

    I stood, stared, and watched as the black clouds moved in; the winds changed direction, summer was over; and you -my new found love, was nothing more than a fainted memory. We held hands in the moonlight, and danced in the dark. We sailed out on the oceans, and built castles in the sand; but, like the tides that came and went - it changed with the season. Standing on the dock, the waters stirred and the little yachts were tossed about like emotions without reason. I couldn't help feeling the loss of the love I thought I had with you.

    But; the winter winds were approaching, and the elms will soon loose their dignity; my thoughts of you - my summer love - will be frozen in time. I dream of you spending thanksgiving; and, catching you walking under the mistletoe; ringing in the midnight with champagne. That was then, and this is "not," what I intended!

Reminiscing where we made love, I stand here - now feeling the freezing winds; the tears streaming down my cheeks and my hands too; trying to keep 'em warm in the fleece of my winter coat. "Oh, God," Do I miss the summer sunsets where we felt the love between us!" And as you wrapped your arms around me; walking down the beach…
Why!" – "Why, did you have to leave?" "I'll never know! God knows though; but, that's not good enough for me! "Why, was I excluded?" "Did I scare you off?" "Did I break your heart?" "Where are you; may I at least, write you a letter?" "I love you - you know?"

    I took a shower, trying to thaw from the freezing cold; remembering, sharing all that's gone. I kneel beside my feathered bed, and ask God for forgiveness! "I'll pray for you!" Tomorrow, I will wake and, "pray!" I hear a knock – maybe. I hope you found, you made a mistake; and, Our Lord gave you the prayer - I prayed. I don't know if you know the love that I felt we created. "Did you feel the same; maybe?" ….

So my Dear Lord, I can only pray that you hear me here, alone --- in my solitude….without you - my love.

Dreams

I suppose we all have times where we think, "If God dreams for us or do, or do we just conjure up dreams on our own?" ... Or is it maybe, we just pray for things to be as we would hope; and, then there are the ones, that only God knows; that start as seeds, and grow in our sub-conscience. But nevertheless, dreams are the desires of life to be as things are not; some situations dampen the ability for the dreams to prosper.

As we sleep like a flower; it grows only in the dark of night! Dreams manifest; and, as a bloom - our dreams become a reality. Never borrowing, that God has His hands on everything that happens; and, then as a new dawn is unfolding, we might remember the last one or two -0 or should we? And then …."What if it's in a prayer that turns into the dream we've been praying for? Confusing --- I think! I try to make sense of dreams I had. Were they our prayers at first; back in the cranium somewhere? Scary!!!

Speaking of which; "what if they are 'nightmares,' which I've been compared to?" The same time; I sit, and wonder, "Am I the answer to the problem; or, "Am I the nucleus to the whole darn thing?" I really shouldn't be compared to where God and your head are on the same pillow. "Don't blame me if your dreams get spoiled!" "It wasn't my doing!".... "Maybe you need to pray - a little harder!!!"

Driving Thru Heaven

In the sweltering summer heat; exhausted, and weary; tired, and impatient - restless from the day; the sun bids a good-bye to another. Before the dark even falls, I have prayed for those in need; and, maybe tomorrow - I'll be closer to the destiny for which I continually pray and dream about. Lying there alone, I close my eyes; and, "Our Father Who Art in Heaven," "Good night!" Somewhere in the twilight; long before dawn, a touch – warm; a palm from a rather large hand saying, "Come!"

Not sure if I had much choice! Should I wake, or just keep dreaming? I was off; no carpet ride, no white horse and chariot; but, a big black 'very long' limousine. Without any notice…I was riding; not driving! "Thank God, I had no idea where I was going." The first thing I noticed was the plant life. Little ferns were broad leafed, and nearly ten feet tall! Then, some elephant ears; tall as a tree, and a stalk like a tree trunk.

Looking ahead, a meadow of oaks the size of redwoods. Scattered amongst flowers; white and yellow, then a field as far as the eye could see! A field only God could have painted; of purple, white, yellow, blue and orange –But! Not a drop of red! … On we drove; thru groves; inquisitive I asked, "Lord why! Why me? … Not a word! Over the hills and into the valleys facing the most exquisite sunset I have ever seen. "Did I mention the sunset was – 360o"

"We passed some gates on the left; white stone columns - they must have been forty feet tall! The entrance read, "Grace Estates!" Yet, we didn't turn; we stayed straight. Again I asked, "Lord" Why me? Where are the people?" Then a dogwood, tall and strong with straight branches; and, the blossoms 'huge and white,' and - not a spec of red! With a turn of His head - and, in a gentle soft voice, He said, "I just thought you might like a sneak peak, "sort of." "No you won't see people!" "It's not your time." But Lord – again –

"Why me?" He smiled; winked; put His hand on my shoulder, and said "Close your eyes!" I did - I woke, dazed, and mesmerized. I thought, "Who can I tell this story to?".... Nobody is going to believe it.....

The Eye of the Needle

I sat in my old truck and watched the moon rise up upside down, mind you. I thought, "I wonder, is this when the ole man sprinkles his dust?" Alone and somber as God is busy blessing others, I waited. The clouds, dark gray against the black of night; the moon is in charge of bringing light from the heavens, the stars give hope; but, they twinkle as they complement the moon in the autumn night ....

And there.....God smiles; the world sighs and rests. The heavens invite those worthy of a place to come and remain with The Lord.... The gates are guarded, the meek are welcome, and those who are blessed find refuge in the kingdom through the "eye of needle"... But I can only wait and ponder; the whole world is in a nut shell, and no one knows tomorrow.

And so it's tomorrow between awakening and dawn and there is peace on earth. No one dies over coffee! It's quiet and tranquil as God intended; and, in these intimate morning moments, love - like moon dust, showers the world. Yes I awake to bless our Savior like a waiter serves, and I am replenished. Though He too enjoys the quiet! His presence is present while sitting here with His feet up, relaxing with me as I write; and, it's these sacred seconds - sharing coffee, and praying for God to bless the fruits of the world; being mindful how our choices inhibit; but, blessings flow; and, God - like a father rules!

So I do as I'm commanded, patiently waiting as there, I too will enter the "eye of the needle."

Eyes of an Old Man

You know - you will never "know," what you will see thru an ole' window!

Today I watched as a wedding went by, it was such a sight. It wasn't long I heard the sounds of sirens, a parade; and, the marching bands. It must be the 4th of July!

It wasn't long and kids had gone back to school again, donned in their brand new clothes; and after school, the streets were filled with sounds of kids as they headed home again.

And then, I saw as I recall - it was fall; the leaves now brown as they lie upon the ground. I watched to see those piles of leaves burn in the cool air. I knew then summer was gone.

Soon it was cold, I know - as I touched that window as it began to snow. It wasn't long I heard bells ring; was it the Holidays again--maybe? It wasn't long, I heard birds sing - must be spring! I sat and thought staring out that ole window.

I watched to see those bare trees. As they sprouted new leaves, it's got to be spring. I touched the glass of that window pane; sure enough it was spring again.

So my days are numbered; and life goes on. I've watched seasons set out over my gated lawn; for I am, too old and lived my life the best I knew how - my wife, gone for some years now. But still I sit and look out, that ole window wondering, will she ever come back to me somehow?

I guess you'll just never know, what you will see -- staring out that ole window.

Finish Line

It was 6 a.m., the sun was making an appearance coming up over the palms. We gathered together, and said a prayer; all 2,500 of us runners Loosening up the joints for a 10k across the brand new 7 mile bridge in the Florida Keys, you couldn't see the other end..... Some quit before they started - for as not to see where they were going because of the curvature of the earth, scared them so badly they wouldn't even start.

Today I think about some acquaintances I have met; and, the lack of faith for one reason or another. There they are – stuck; can't trust where life might take them; they remain, like standing on Hwy A1A afraid to run the marathon. Though, God gives us faith to build and go on, blinded to the future; afraid from the past. "We hold on - to what?" "Nothing! --- It's gone..... Even today, a beautiful breezy Monday; and, got a lot accomplished to say the very least. Its over!!!

Should we lie in fear as we say our prayers, or keep the faith that God knows what He's doing? For tonight…even I pray for all I know; that God will lead them down a path of happiness and joy; not fear, or stress and sorrow - tomorrow...

Yes it's so sad that as life has pitched a curve to you; it's no reason to quit, just because you hit a foul ... I wonder.... I know death has played a role in some ways, to us all; but, you know those gone, "Would they want you to stop living; or, put on you running shoes, and get back in the marathon? For whatever the reason; ... you stopped; ask yourself, "Am I sinning? "There's a thought ... not doing as God would want ...

 "The finish line," the opposite end of the beginning --where there you can stop; and, the biggest sin in all of this…

... "You didn't even try!" "Sadly!!!"...

Fish Bowl

There at the corner of Sax and Fifth Ave. - Christmas shopping for family and friends; it's snowing with five days left to go; wondering what I could get you, something special - maybe something from Neiman Marcus! Looking up to watch the street light, the snow was falling - the buildings towering from above; disappeared in the clouds as I was - waiting to cross.

Looking up I thought about how minute I am, wandering from store to store; remembering shopping together with you in years past; but you're home, and I'm here on an assignment working for an investment company. Nonetheless, looking at the thousands of busy shoppers, I feel like I'm in a fish bowl trying to survive; a barrage of others trying to do the same thing! It's like swimming upstream to spawn… "What a frenzy!"

Trying to find that memorable remembrance, the holiday is fast approaching; but, the battle isn't in the malls – it's on the streets as its survival of the fittest that claims us all right here in the crossroads of this fish bowl.

Stopping for a cappuccino, I thought about my life as I write trying to succeed - getting ahead, isn't an option! A must, watching the competition out there, trudging in the falling snow; but here in this fish bowl, my every move is scrutinized. My routines watched, my actions – judged! In the middle of downtown New York - the crossroads inviting me, I remain diligent to My Lord above, trying not to let the competition get me down. For in this world of "dog-eat-dog," I - sitting here at this cafe, only have to answer to myself, and the Lord above.

I just pray - I'm blessed and my efforts aren't in vain, and some day .... maybe -- they'll change the water.....in this old fish bowl...... I pray! ...

Footprints

There on a hot afternoon, I met you where the sea oats and sand, accompanied the landscape to a back drop in beautiful sea foam green. As I was walking over the dune, only God could have known that there on the other side approaching me, was a woman of incredible distinctions. Her brunette curls whispered in the wind, and as you took your hand to wipe your hair out of your face, a towel thrown over you exposing just enough to tell the sun had kissed you by the sea - your little cut-off jeans left little doubt that you had enough of the sun for a day. Coming down the dune watching you as you were climbing the other side watching me, a smile on your face as you approached.

"Afternoon," I said, or so I thought; and, I heard you, "Howdy." I stopped, "Had enough," smiling - you looked at me; "Cooked," was all you said. We spoke a minute or so more, as I was headed to the shore. You were nothing more than a passing thought.

Walking in the shallows - refreshed by the coolness, I thought about the encounter I had, and just how gorgeous you were. Now bored from the loneliness, I decided to leave; crossing the dunes listening to the weeds, climbed into my truck and headed west.

Staring in the sun trying to see – was that a mirage? "Could it be?" "It was!" --- You were walking up the street. I stopped, "Can I give you a lift?" "Oh please, my feet are killing me." I watched as you slipped off your sandals… "May I put my feet up for just a minute?" "Certainly," was all I said; and, continued to drive you to your condominium?

The next day came and I was determined to find you again. I pulled out of the underground lot, and there in the glare, you had left your footprint on my windshield. I thought - how wonderful to have a memory where you had been if only for a brief moment in time.

And, as God allows us to have encounters throughout life; its climbing up and over the dunes where we find life, love, and - maybe even happiness.

Fortunately

Today I pray for those less fortunate; the ill, the lame and those who have to work. Sadly as so many feel as though God has forgotten their dreams and prayers, they move away from the center. I watched the dampness as the sun sparkled on the petals, rejuvenated by the rays of warmth; where in the night - only darkness. The flowers are forgotten and the cool temps with little promise, they too spring, and smile to be alive when the morning comes.

For God has not forgotten what makes a flower achieve their beauty, nor has He left you there wilt in the summer heat. Like the trees - as the flowers; He replenishes all His living creatures. Here where there is breathe, life persists; and, all good comes from deep within the spirit; a smile like a flower, a sparkle too in our eye. God in the darkest moments has not forgotten – you!

I watch you too, knowing He is. I see the light that shines in your heart, the rays that come straight from the heavens. No, it's not unfortunate; but, fortunate for you the Lord stands guard, waiting for your command; and, as peace falls like leaves, harmony comes to your heart.

For there in the spirit, may God be your healer as He promises spring to the flowers. Never doubt the love I have for you as our Father in Heaven leans against the gate, smiling down..... Waiting..... Waiting for you to come to the center.....

Gifts

It's been a long day! Went to church twice, repeatedly thanking God for my life – content. I talked to my love, and shared some thoughts about God's grace. She said, "You're so lucky!" Humbly - I said, "Honey it's a gift!" Everyone has gifts, some never find them. Yes - that maybe; but nonetheless, God gives us all gifts; some to be funny, some to invent, some to preach, some to make money, and some just to set a good example. Mine may be to write; but, I'm not sure yet.

One thing I have learned, "gifts" come from above; and, those who have found that special one, are too – gifted, as our dear Lord has blessed them from above with the ultimate gift; "Love!" Happily driving home from church, I watched as the sun said good bye; there behind the clouds as though it had pulled the covers up over its shoulders, it bid me a good night. It's been a wonderful day to be alive.

Tomorrow will be here soon enough; and, obligations to fulfill, deadlines to meet; and, money changes hands. With all that, our electric life we lead - God I know now, must be first. So, finding comfort from leaving church is now a way of life; and, not mandatory as some would lead you to believe; but, loving life is part of God!

As you bow your head and say your prayers, remember, "It's only our Lord that makes those dreams come true; and before you close your eyes --- smile! You're blessed. Thank God you're alive! Amen.

God's Art

Tonight in the light of dark, I see the final chapter that God has permitted me to write for as God instructed us to love, and to forgive, to share the gifts we all have within – all with each other as we may be better in Gods eyes than to sit alone, and wither to dust; where our breathing bones turn to shaded stones, there on a deserts' floor; and, love falls short where life is left in morning.

In the crisp cloudless sunset, answers appear from the heavens. We are born the same; and, we all fall short of the glory - even though we still praise him, and magnify his name; but, as sinners - we are all the same.

Wrapped in our own little worlds we have created; making sure our comforts are convened. I watch! "Do we really share?" "Are we there to help or, is it just sympathy?" As we all learn from messages, and apply them to our everyday…I look and watch those close to me. I know and see the implication --- hasn't taken hold; I regret that love as a word, has been so abused. It's a noun, or is it a verb? Giving was the old testaments description; but, "Do we really; or, are we focused with the day-to-day grind; and, could care less if 'love' is ever shared." So many promises we make, and our devotion to them – gone; for love - a noun….a possession. We all have fallen into a trap where, what is - maybe - what is not?

I think about those "life -long" marriages of devotion… "Were they in love; or, are you putting in time…servicing a commitment? And, when it's done - do we not continue giving - I wonder. Even a tiny candle - gives of itself - Our biblical ways of living are just reading and agreeing - certainly can't expect us today to live by those same standards …or, should we?

"Giving" the gift; a gift of love, not intimately at all - being nice, friendly, courteous, and kind; that's what God wants from us. Think how wonderful it would be - to be let in the traffic line, instead of being cut off; or, someone to hold the door as your hands are full; and, you're trying not to drop everything.

Yes I pray, the day will come when we treat everyone like our own. I pray for the day we all find that love we have prayed for, year after year. And for those who have lost after many years of marriage; understand God's got plans for you - so don't stop living!!! ---- Amen.

God's Stage

Like on cue, I rose to see the moon as it disappeared from view. I stared - only wished I had your hand to hold on to; sharing this moment that only passes once in a great while. Where the earth and the heavens open up; and, God lets us get a snap shot of his majestic beauty. I watched, I listened as the earth was humbled in honor of Him; and, His ever present command to make the moon disappear as the sun had fully lit - what our eyes watched Him do.

And as if that wasn't enough, like a play on the big stage to watch; there, shooting through the heavens was a star with a trail a hundred miles long lighting up the night - directed by God for believers to see that only He was able to deliver this enormous display of cosmic gorgeousness. Still, as astrologers map and calculate the next time they think this will happen; it's only our Lord that can do the math, and put a little zing in the equation, as we remain mesmerized, watching.

Oh dear Lord, such power and grace; a combination not worthy of mortal man. A relentless strength that's only "You," we honor; and, as the moon slowly reappears, the moonlight gives presence to a cloud that wasn't there...where an angel stands. "Was she there the whole time, or was she just caught in the act of helping God?" I wonder! .....I smiled for we have just witnessed a little of God's humor.

Yes, and of all the starry songs that have ever been written; none could depict this one, where God gave to us living proof that He lives! There alone, I pray, "Did you arise to see the heavens in action, or was it you that the trail of dust was sprinkled in the middle of the night? I sent you a wish as it passed over me..... "I love you - did you get it...?!"

God's Timing

There in the moonlight; I watched, thinking… "Hmmmm!," - the sun must be late; it should be shining! The stars poised as they too are waiting to rest from their night's hard work - twinkling. Even the birds, perched on the branches, like waiting on the Olympics to begin; but, not a sound did they make...

Doing my usual in the morning, I too waited and watched; "Is God's timing late, I wondered?" I thought, "If God made the earth in seven days; why can't I build a house in that amount of time? So, maybe God watches His own stop watch, just to see how fast he can create.

There in the speed of light as The Son rose, God's timing is His own; teaching us patience; and, to trust in Him as the future is, "His, only." I twisted my arm, checking to see, if maybe mine and Gods are in-sync. "Do we ever know?" "Yes!" I think when harmony, day after day flows from one's heart to others; like trees, painted the landscape in living color; living in harmony together ..... I smile!

In the communion of morning; God offers time for us to be creative as well, through gifts of His; we are called! It's our duty to love and to serve as we watch our watches; ever mindful that the beauty of both, are what makes us different; and "giving," keeps us in check like setting your watch when you're a little late; remembering that giving is the nucleus of time ....Amen ..

God's Vestibule

I woke and went to watch the waves; there as they kissed the shore, the foam looked like snow; had it been a lot colder; the sand, lined in white, sparkled in the sun. I watched the terns as they ran around the foam; their little legs running a hundred miles an hour. I wondered, "Why don't they just spread their wings? But instead, they seem to play, scooping up anything that comes by them. They chased the frothy bubbles left on the sand like buried treasure--they'd investigate.

The whole flock lifted; and, gliding over the edge, kept a birds-eye as the waves were coming in for fasting from the night. "I guess - was their instinctive thought" "I watched them as they too, kept eye on me." "After all, I was in their domain!"
And as the sun warmed the earth; looking out, a school porpoise crested the surface. I thought to myself, "God, what a harmonic balance as are all things are created by "You."

"I watched as even the sound of the surf, so invigorating"… "Hmmmm." "What if it made a different sound? "Would we still be drawn where the gentle winds; the peaceful shore; the life, above and; there below; with me on the beach staring. "Wow God! What a spectacular scene!

There - where "Grace" is all about you; a sanctuary of life; that we are allowed to share; and, enjoy the beauty. "Oh my Lord, how blessed we are; thankful as the sun reflects off the rolling swells, blessed to be alive; and, to come to you at….. "Your vestibule!"

God's Watching

    The noise from next door eluded me of a circumstance in turmoil that I felt it necessary to intercede. I knocked on the door. "May I come in?" Then a loud "NO!!" Persistent, I knocked and said you either let me in, or I'll call the cops….if it will make you feel better. The door cracked open, not exactly the welcoming committee I was hoping for.

Strewed across the room were toys and baby bottles; and, pouting - standing in the corner, was the cutest strawberry blonde sniffing her heart out. I went to touch and comfort her. Her father said, "Don't touch her." I put my hand on her little shoulder. She turned her head, and instantly reached out for me to hold her. I picked her up and asked her; "How old are you?" She mumbled – "twue." I said, "Dear God - where is the love?" She wrapped her arms around my neck, like a choke hold – almost; as I held her, I prayed, "Father in heaven forgive him, for he (her father) knows not ... Now not a sound, not a whimper, not a cuss word was mentioned for God in his infinite power had calmed everything. "Thank you – Jesus," I thought; then God spoke – "I'm watching you," "Me?" "Yes, it is I that has bequeathed of you, to honor my children with the same love as I have for you." Flattered and humbled, I took that two year old, and sat her on my lap. "You hungry?" "Uh huh," she said. Going to the stove - hot dogs on boil, I reached in bare handed and retrieved one for her. Her father watching, "Are you crazy?"

"No," I said. She needs to eat! I looked at her and said "let's pray." Not knowing what that meant…somehow on my lap, she bowed her head. "Heavenly Father, bless this food to her use." We took turns blowing to cool the hot dog, and as I fed her little nibbles, she smiled and asked me, "Who is God?" I smiled, and tried to explain that God is the one you pray to when you're sad or in tears; He is there for you; He brought you, "me," - matter of fact!" Yes, God is watching you too, I explained. I put her down, now happier and full. I stood up and took her father by the arm, "Let's talk, shall we?" Stepping out to the porch I turned, and said, "Do you go to church?" He hung his head. This was enough of an answer for me. I leaned over, and wrapped my arm around his shoulder and said, "Son, you must believe!" "God's watching you," and if you don't believe, you would have never seen me do what I did. He looked up, and in query- he said, "Calm my daughter" "No," ... I stick my hand in the boiling water.

Gone Fishing

Early on a Saturday morn, I took my canoe to the end of the dock; tied it up, and headed back to the truck to get the rest of my stuff. A cool damp fall morning, I couldn't believe it was the middle of summer; but I gathered my gear, and walked back down to the dock, threw it in the canoe; set my coffee cup on the pier, got in, grabbed my cup, untied the canoe, and casted off.

I paddled off into the fog or haze, whatever it was - It was far from burning off. The sun was nothing but a dim glare above, as the sky was cold; remained dark, lifeless, and I was the only thing that dared in the morning light. I didn't go far in the dark from where I launched; around the point was far enough.... So I grabbed my rod and casted out, lay on the gunnels; and, drifted, sipping on my coffee.

There in the solitude of the waters, I pondered. I looked to the stars; there weren't any! - Still too foggy; but, looking up, I asked myself, "Has life for so many, become a sport of chance in happenstance, where we never know what's swimming by the hook; and, what if a fish shod take the bait? Then what...... And there, I ask the Lord, "Is this where I should be - I don't even like to fish?" "Where are you heading me?" With that, my rod moved. I grabbed before it went into the water; then in the peace of the early morn, I heard a laugh; but, I was too far from shore to hear someone ...., or was it.... He? ... I laughed as well!" You think this is funny - don't you?"...... Then – nothing!!! Not even a nibble. Was the bait gone? Trying to comprehend... "Was God trying teach me something of which I know not; fishing you know is not my forte'; but, patience has left a lot to be desired. That needs lots of work!"

Watching the sun as it quietly rose, not wanting to disturb a soul; the dark came to life, full of color. The fog now gone as the sun burned it off. I started to paddle to another location. I casted again, and watched my rod as it rested on the gunnels; poured another cup coffee and waited. Then, as if the heavens opened, God spoke. "If you don't like to fish, then why are you up, out here so early?" Half scared, I sat up..... My Lord in heaven, "What is it that you bequest?" Then my rod started to jiggle. I grabbed it again, and jerked as hard as I could; and, as I fought this fish to bring it to the top, He said, "We all must never quit!" "What do you mean," He replied, "Life?" - "Life?" What do you mean – life?"

Then dead silence, and even the fish was gone as well. Stumped, I dumped my coffee, and started to paddle back. Then I heard, "You quit!" I said, "Sure, why not?" Now half disgusted, the Lord appeared in bow of my canoe. "Oh my God, " I thought. He heard my thought, "Yes, it's me." He said, "Please don't stop ...." I looked Him right in the eye, and said "Stop life!" "What in the world is going on?" "What are you talking about?"...

He smiled and said, "Son, it's always darkest right before the dawn; "And? – Your point being," I replied. The world is full of disappointment; but, as you turn your boat to the wind, cast - let not "you" be discouraged; for it's only me that will see you through your troubled waters. And then, he vanished. I asked myself, "Did that really happen?" "What's in this coffee - I'm drinking?"

Next week I went back to the same spot; but, He was not ... and then - there I learned what He meant! ..... For life can pass you by once or twice; but, if you believe in Him as you repeatedly try...

"Cast!" - With God you will succeed.....

Goodbye

    A cold cloudy Sunday, snow impending soon; the shades of gray, say the weatherman might be right; but, today as I thought in church about the pastor's words, realizing that for every "hello" there will be a "good-bye." Though good-byes are so hard; knowing the destination is as impending as the snow. We are ever reminded, that the journey we travel has brought us thus far; and, for that of which we are, has been instilled. That we are a product of our past; and, to say "good-bye" is giving in, not giving up! Our change in life is - where we are; and so, "What we do to preserve our sanity…for 'good-bye' is permanent……."The End!"

This isn't the end; but, the other end where it begins. It's not the destination we seek; but, the journey we enjoy, as we walk through this world pray'n. God accompanies us through happiness; strife, or "whatever" life has to offer. I looked at you with disbelief, yet joy came over me from above.

"Joy - the 'Joy of The Lord' is your strength!" Nehemiah 8:10

    So is there joy in goodbye; "Yes," but not as you would imply from peace from within. Goodbye to a deceased… "Joy - your strength --- where we come to meet disbelief, strife, grief all rolled into "One."

    But then as Pastor bespoke of heritage; and, what we inherited or did not; we to need to say good-bye; change our legacies of life; begin when we start to take another journey with God; and, only then we realize that life as we know it, was not as it seems.

    So say good-bye; go ahead – it's okay; for "going forward" is leaving some things in your life behind; and, "It's okay; but realize –"JOY follows through God."

    I am far from a scholar; or even one to look to; but, my spirit; and, my faith which have allowed me to share my thoughts with you - - "My love; my hope - I pray! My words bring you a gift that only comes by our God, above. Amen!

Grains of Sand

Early on a Saturday dawn, I sat alone on the beach, and watched the ocean; like a sheet of glass, it was still asleep. I only, was privileged to capture what I saw! As the amber crested the horizon, the earth had paused - reverently almost; not even a bird in sky, no sounds at all! I whispered, "Lord?" "Good morning!" "I know you're here!" "You've calmed the ratchet ocean waters from the stormy seas of the night before." Not even a ripple on the beach as I watched as far as my naked eye could see, nothing; but, a sheet of glass mirroring off toward the heavens.

Quietly, staring off …a movement in the sand; a little crab had dug his way out venturing, looking at me. I smiled, and thought, "Now this is truly a stand-off." I'm watching this tiny guy, and he has swallowed a giant eyeful of me. Oh Lord, your humor is resiliently breath taking! To have this little crab looking like he's going to attack me, as if I'm on his private property - how hilarious is this! To show him who's boss, I sprinkled a little sand on top of him, and off he went; maybe to pick on somebody his own size, hopefully.

The sun half crested and a magnificent display of rays; purple and green; red and yellow, refracted through the hazy humidity. Quietly still, I sat in a trance – almost. I wonder why it's only I that God has allowed to sit here in His theatre and watch the morning views. A tap on the shoulder…"Was it The Lord, I thought… and, in a soft romantic voice, "I brought you a cup of coffee." I turned and looked, my trance turned into reality. Looking up at you, I spoke. "Oh honey, sit and enjoy the final scenes of this spectacular morning." Rubbing the sand off each other's toes; and, embracing the morning warmth, sipping our coffee while a school of porpoise were combing the shores looking for breakfast; we smiled and watched as their fins cut the water like a knife, black dorsal fins piercing the surface; but not even a ripple did they make – they too not wanting to disturb the beauty.

My eye catches a little movement in the sand again. I nudge you, "Look!" staring between my bent knee, holding my cup with both hands; a little sand crab approaches, raises up, and spits some sand at me. I laughed…. No, I rolled! You looked at me, "What's so funny?" "Oh, my love …you just had to be here to catch the first scenes of this incredible morn!"

Grandma's Rocker

Looking back when I was young; I had it good, you might say. My mom worked and took me to the safest place – here on earth; it was here, I rocked in grandma's arms in her big ole' rocker.

As I grew, I used to stew, and rock away; thinking about the things that might someday come my way. I wished and dreamed, what I wanted to be; but, it was there in grandma's rocking chair – that's where I found me!

It wasn't long before I found myself in puberty; my feet now touched the ground; and, as I sat in her rocking chair; I had grown, and she was gone – yet, I knew as I grew "here" would always be a place for me - in Grandma's rocking chair!

Soon I had a son, and never thought that rocking him would mean so much! It calmed him down – every time, as though she was still there, in great grandma's rocking chair.

As the generations passed, the rocking chair is still around; even after all these many years. The kinfolk still take their turn in Grandma's rocking chair.

But - just yesterday, I almost gave away Grandma's old rocking chair. My family cried, for I had tried to give away the only thing that kept us all here, together as a family "Grandma's Old Rocking Chair!"

Here

New shoes that killed my feet; and, a new shirt's collar that irritated the fire out of my neck, I was being dragged down isle as mom wanted to show me off to the entire congregation! Shoved me in the pew; and, about broke my arm as she made me sit down, right where she wanted me to. My brother on the other hand, limped along quietly and dared not get out of line. So there we were - in the second row from the front, spit and polished; mom in her painted skirt and matching shawl; and, her pill box with some baby's breath donning her new white gauntlets. I couldn't tell if it was the pew or the starch in my shorts that hurt. I tried to wiggle, but she slapped my knee. Finally we stood! That felt better! The preacher spoke, "Let us pray!" Mom held my hand like, "you move - I'll break your fingers".

But in those days, we learned to "hold hands" with friends we never knew, and sometimes I got to hold the hand of a little blond that captured my heart on Sunday morn.

And as I grew, holding hands was a tradition we all loved to do. Going through life light years ahead of where I use to be, today I stood where I have for too many years; wishing I had the love that honored the value of standing beside me, holding my hand in church as God watches to see the pain where reminiscing has been alone.

Yet back in the day, I remember our entire church prayed together; and, we held each other's hands; and, we gave thanks to God no matter the circumstances! Together, we prayed....Amen..

Here's Where I Am

    I sat here in the peace of darkness for only me, and "thee" were present. I heard the "hmmm" of the air conditioner; but, waited on His word. The sanctuary was full – so full of unanswered prayers; hopes, and dreams as so many come to see if God hears them as well. I take my place, and lean against the side board. Paused to see if "He" is here, maybe waiting on me as well.

    The lights come up; still not a sound. "Did He hear me?" "Did He know I was here waiting too; in the clutches of my memory - I put myself in neutral. I think about my past, and then "Where is God leading me? The bright lights look like a brand new morning as the sanctuary is fully lit; but, no one knows that I am sitting here, waiting on the message.

Dead tired; overwhelmed, frustrated, and exhausted, for I alone will never be able to conquer my quest, not without the help of Jesus.... So I come to where we meet, and "here" on many occasions; I walk away renewed in my spirit; if it only would last longer than a day or two. Too many altercations to deal with at one time, maybe....

    But without fail as promised; He reaches out and grabs the very root of my soul, and reminds me like so many others that faith is always being remodeled. As a sculptor surely improves from the last, we too are molded to fit all that God wants of us. Silently in all the light, it's my Lord showing me the way to find the faith I need to penetrate what I can't see.

And then the piano, a carousel of heavenly notes begins to fill the air. A peace reigns, still - the only one here to enjoy that which God has given to me ... "Joy " if nothing else for the happiness I have, and love to share; will keep me here in my solitude, from this day forward till we - He and me, meet right here again..... Amen!....

Hey God Ya got a Sec

    There early on a Monday morn; my alarm forgot to sound. Now running out of time, and confronting the traffic jam that surely comes, driving through for coffee - - -"Gosh, I got to get gas!!!" I hit the clock. It's ten after and I greeted the boss coming around the corner. Heard he had a wreck on the way to work; guess he caused the jam that made me late. Grabbing my second cup sitting at my desk; I took a deep breath, and closed my eyes asking, "Hey, God --- got a sec?" Before you know it, time to quit --- back to the rat race, go pick up kids from day care; help the older ones with homework; make dinner; PTA; check on parents in the nursing home; kid's baths; shower, and then - maybe wind down before you start tomorrow. Finally….crawl in bed; pull the covers up; kiss your spouse, and close your eyes - saying to yourself.... "Hey God --- got a sec?" ....

Tomorrow will be here before you know it, and as you drift off with heavy lids, you pray, "Hey God --- got a sec;" and, as you pray, He hears you pour out your heart ….. Searching your soul…"God, make me better; heal me, Father; heal my body where no Band-Aid can cover. I pray, I sleep, and tomorrow be better...

    In the light of night…angels surround your spirit, and replenish your defenseless heart. Unguarded, angels have heard your prayers; healing your body as you sleep; restoring your strength…you'll need it in the morning; "Yes," as you lay helpless; God in fact, has time for you; not only listening, but caring for you too. As dawn awakens the weary, you stretch and yawn, and feel rested; a smile comes where yesterday you panicked. "Oh yes," God's got a sec for you – alright!!!

The trick, you know --- is just praying! He'll get around to you - I'm sure; just as soon as He gets through with me!!! .... :)

Him, He, Mom and Me

There I stare at the tarnished old silver frame lying in bed, "looking." "It occurred to me, were there three, or was there four, in that old picture sitting on top of my dresser drawers. My brother six, mom was maybe twenty-seven and me a mere eighteen months, being held in her arms as my brother's smile "lights up" the picture.

My mom stood with head tilted slightly, and me - probably praying she didn't drop me. It's a handsome picture to be sure; but, it's the one - you cannot see that I miss the most! Yes, there behind the glass, and out of view; behind the lens, taking the picture; my father, six-two, ex-navy pilot from World War II, stood there quietly trying to make sure the shutter worked for all the family to see; and, enjoy for years to come.

I lost him at the age of fourteen; some stupid eating disorder killed him! Today, he would have been well up in his nineties. But you know, the memories live on - even though, he didn't. I lay there starring at the man who took the picture; my father who art in heaven, the legacy lives on in the pride he portrayed as "in his footsteps," I try to carry on. "Yes, I guess - those were the days when family ties kept us together - There reminiscing, staring at the family portrait "one's missing."

It was "him" I needed in my life, now gone from view; and, out of the picture. Mom remarried; but, it was still "him" I missed the most; and, now today - I wonder where I would have been, had he lived a little longer! I shutter, thinking.

Photo of Dana!

Homage

There while listening to the morning news, straightening up from night before. I picked up the blanket that you were wrapped in having coffee. I held the blanket to my face to see if there might be a hint of your fragrance remaining. I wrapped my arms around that minty green soft attire that you wore for your morning cup, I stopped and paid "homage" to the love I knew was gift wrapped like a delicacy longing to be served; but then as before, you had to leave - gone! .....like buried treasure from my back yard, here today, and well you know that story.

Yet I stood there at the foot of the bed , and balled up the blanket into my arms , " I love you " I thought to myself , but only God could hear me; and, as I stowed my minty green comforter, I thought how sad to hide this marvelous treasure like valuables out in the yard, were none would ever know. Never knowing about the memories we made and that they grew when you were alone in my presence.

And looking up a day later sat your coffee cup on my table, where you left it, a tribute to your presence in memory maybe. So there I stared and thought, "God, is this love?" "Is this what love is - to bury what you treasure; and, hide it from all to see?" "I can't believe that's what God wants. But facts remain that there are so many relationships that are demolished and ruined, because - as you know, things you bury - deteriorate, and can't exist without a daily dose of sun and love. As God gives to His flowers to bloom, love needs the same, to be nurtured daily!

So today I pray, "God, where is the love I'm supposed to have?" "Where is the happiness, the joy being buried like gold in the back yard with all the love Jesus showed? It wasn't a lesson to learn! "No!" it was and is a way of life. I sit and think when will that love; that way of life; "Will I be blessed with?" ......

Honest to God

I listened to the early dawn, awakened by gentle sounds as you lie fast asleep, peacefully dreaming. I got up and poured a cup of two day old orange something or another; and, went into a state where prayer was ever-lasting; for only answers are delivered like overnight mail; praying about you, for only He knew the truth, as I worshipped you.

But clouded in a mask like putting on makeup in the morning, I watched you; and, as you start out of the house, I reclined to pray. Today you may go to honor the highest, and be… "Honest to God," to be delivered from evil, for Satan waits like perked coffee .....

Wondering, may today - you be delivered from the anxiety of truths unknown, where broken hearts pave the way to tomorrow; and, as our creator bequests of us to stay beside Him, and never leave his right; we find ourselves stumbling in the valley, clouded, and rainy; lost in confusion, troubled by trusts. I pondered in your presence, knowing your spirit had too been broken; and, love - with limits - a design flaw - was not by God's design!

Afterwards you leave; and, as you do, you share with the family. It's there that happiness and joy reaches out to sooth your wavering spirit. Oh, I do pray you are - "Honest to God," and blessings flow in His holy name! Be healed, for life prospers like wild flowers on mountains; for only God may bring your heart to a safe harbor.

Horizons

With my head propped on my pillow; the fan hums with a gentle breeze, the clock in the kitchen ticking away second by second. I'm waiting - lying awake. I wonder under the covers as my mind is at a crossroads, for my love is lost; and, I remain! I stood on the balcony and called her name….

.Where, Dear Lord - is this love you promised?

Day after day, I pray to be with the keepsake you promised; but, still today - - - I stand alone; and, at this moment in time, I focus where the future leads me. As the sun came up, challenging with new horizons; I decide I'll go get a cup of coffee, and sit out on the porch as always. I'll listen to the little birds, and see if they can direct me; and, so Lord - I sit, and sip my coffee, patiently waiting like a chess game; watching and waiting to make my next move for God presents opportunities – choices; I'm left at the balcony of life, looking down to where I've been; and, able to see possibilities as the future leads me.

By His grace; I go to destinations unknown. But, I know… I'm not alone, for He leads me… I follow. Alone, praying this journey will soon end.

If Time Stood Still

I pulled the covers up over you - the sun was nowhere in the heavens; for there I looked, and stared saying, "Lord, I wish this moment could last forever!" The clock now read 4:13. I rolled to hold the love of my dreams. "Please, Lord - if it's possible; stop the clock, and, let me hold onto the most precious lady here on earth." There in the dark - an angel came down from the heavens; and said, "I'm here to grant your request.... for our Lord spoke - be with them as they lie in peace." ....Quietly, we held - time passed with my arms around you, questioning the happening. I turned my head to look once more - and sure enough - 4:13 was what my little clock on my night stand said. --

I looked to heaven, there - still holding you, "Thank you – Jesus, for these moments we share." "You gave to me more than I deserve. "Thank You again for loving us;" and, then - like that, as quick as she came - without a sound, and not even goodbye; she rose to where she came....

Still embracing, it was 4:28; with your head on my pillow, starring at each other - you whispered, "Am I to believe what I just witnessed?" I chuckled, grinned, and kissed you on your head saying, "My dear, you can doubt it if you want; but, you heard - and saw the same as I - can't deny that… now can you?...

Magically as we stayed in the clutches of each other, the sun's rays blasted through the blinds. Squinting over your shoulder, I guess it's time to get up!... For God came, and blessed us; sent an angel to stand over us, and then He wished both of us a good day with a beam of light to brighten up our day.....

Illusions

"So, let me ask you," "What is an illusion?" "Is it thoughts passed from you of things now gone from view?" "Are they just circumstances that interrupt your day; and, by tomorrow are gone away? Or, "Are we just a brief flash in time that too soon will be gone?" "Are - we - the illusion of life?"

So I turned to where I thought the answers would come. Searching my soul, I asked God - are these events I encounter are an illusion too. - But they hurt as they too are gone from view; and, "How can I tell if they're real or not," I wonder as I sit. "Does memory play a part, for things now lost or gone; are now, only a photo that hangs in your heart.

"Yes." I too - have memories, thoughts of things past - as you; but, they're gone too as we stand here – alone, and try to recall those that are gone. "Do you remember?" "Maybe, you do." "Did it really happen?" Why didn't it last…forever - as God does in you?" But…I came to a corner - where life takes a turn. "Is faith an illusion of things unknown?" So much of my life, I see is in a rear view mirror it seems to me; but, as faith has given us opportunity to proceed; illusions of lives past, remain.

Not understanding the complicated question – "Why?" I have no answer. It's only God, who can supply "the why!" We are here, hurt; tears in our eyes. The illusion of love once shared looking down; we observe then commemorate the illusion of what was - once. It is now too - gone from view!

So today as the sun brings a smile upon your face, let not that smile - be an illusion to cover your heart as it too tries to smile inside of you - out of view. God has only given us just "so many" days, to make it right; and, be a part of His master plan…Illusions to us! "Yes," "Maybe!" – But, we are all connected to the illusion of life.

"Should we just give up?" I ask. "I think not, for God won't be very proud of me if I take away the illusion He wants to see in me." "Trust, your faith is no illusion!!!

In the Blink of an Eye

Another normal day there; or, so you think! The sun's rays are burning away the dampness of the morning dew; the bird rejoices in the cloudless sky; people let you in for a change, as you try to merge from lane to lane. The world is perfect as it continues to spin. But then the news comes, it's a stint or its terminal; and, "in the blink of eye;" the world changed for you as situations and thoughts become predominant.

What once seemed so important, don't mean a damn now! Priorities aren't important somehow as life has just robbed you! "Living 'till your ninety" is now a pipe dream of "make-believe." Sadly, it's just not your world that gets rocked; but, friends and family; acquaintances you've barely met; and, new neighbors next door. You can't explain what's happening to you… to them!

And as the tulip tree still grows in spite of the draught; standing straight, and tall - all on its own, God gives it another chance at life..... Humbly, thanking God for a second chance - where if it were for not our Lord, dust to dust; it would be the last! In spite of the consequences, we remain vigilant to our cause as in that - God blesses us all!

As we lay in our beds at night, and watch the sunsets; we ask, "Why," yet gracious are we for the continuance; it's the "how come," we continue to seek; and there in a "blink of an eye," our world is turned upside down….rocked by the unexpected, for it is our God that gives us the strength to journey on. As precious as life may be, even a little tulip tree persists as we watch the moon crest!

In Tune

    I'm not much of a concert goer. In fact, I've relished myself not to be present if I could help it; but tonight, upon request, I went with you to hear the vibrant sounds of music. Filing in - I heard the instruments warming up; and, grumbling from the floor as on-lookers were trying to find a seat to see the orchestra. As the crowd grew, sitting elbow to elbow, I thought how partnerships feel as close – then becomes a discomfort; but, we waited and listened.

    There as our patience tempered, the lights finally dimmed; and, the draped curtains opened. I was ready to move for being uncomfortable with the crowd - there was little I could do. Anticipation grew - but then, the first few bars of soothing notes made me feel like I was watching Mozart; and, as the orchestra performed versions of some modern day classic hits; it dawned on me, "Why can't we all live like an orchestrated symphony in our hearts? And as thoughts arose, the music enticed my adrenalin; it brought thoughts of love like relationships "ought to be - - - a symphony"... "In tune," where the harmony and tones, spread the sounds of love like winds across the waters....

    And at my age, pains run together - seem to keep rhythm with the times - I've had a few close calls where our hearts were in harmony; just a little off key! But for me - the unexpected like tightening a guitar string; the pitch is perfect. We love, and in our hearts, sing. For God has composed a combination of sweet eloquent sounds as we harmonize, and share from within our hearts. But, there in the concert hall, I held your hand as the music coming from down within - resonated. We clapped, and applauded the band. What a great job of bringing us all together; for there like life, a little practice - and we all can make music, keeping step with the time….

    As our hearts may beat differently, we - together - provide a rhythm where a symphony creates the music; life and love grow instrumentally within ourselves; cherishing the melody, the joy it brings, where life, and God - you and me - we sing, giving praises, as we may create our own little symphony.

Inspiration

It was Wednesday, noon or so as I walked into the room. There, entombed…barely breathing, almost comatose lay a little lady beyond recognition. Her head swollen; her eyes shut and blackened; her left arm slung as if it was broken; and, enough electrical! I thought …..She was on life support?

Quietly as I thought she was sleeping, I leaned to kiss her hand lying lifeless upon the sheets. "Kathy?" "Hi honey… it's me!" "Do you know I am?" As lifeless as seemed possible, she nodded her head. Alone, I asked God to protect this child; give her strength that comes from – You! I stood guard as to make sure my prayers were answered; I held her lifeless hand as I bent over to kiss her forehead; which was all that showed. "God bless you" I said as she squeezed my fingers. I knew I became her inspiration to live! I prayed a moment or two more; chatted with a nurse monitoring her vitals from the station on the floor; and, said my goodbyes.

The next few days I ran away at lunch, to see if there was anything I could do to help; and, every day, I saw a little progress. But there, unbeknownst to me lie a little lady whose whole life revolved around my visit, showing her vitals placate on my merely arriving. Her children knew I was her inspiration; and, I understood in faith and hope; a lifeless lady was fixing dinner and bathing her dogs only the night before; and as her spirit lie dormant, it was "I" that brought her promise.

There as fragile is; the mere existence of life maybe, it's not faith or hope that saves; but, inspiration that soothes the soul and calms the spirit.

Islands

There in the waters up to my knees; I turned, and looked back to see if I see the whole island that stood behind me. And as I looked to the right, the cool blue gave way to the palms in the sand; and, the motion as the breeze filtered through the fronds. Following up to the clear blue of the mountain tops; majestically they stood alone, unshaken by what the weather for thousands of years had thrown. My eyes followed the topography to where driftwood lay in memory of past hurricanes on the weathered side; sadly I realize that this little island may not be a match for Mother Nature at all!

I stood in the sparkling blue, and thought about how you too have resisted; trying to withstand the wrath and fury of life, alone... like this little piece of paradise, so inviting; yet incapable to reach out for support; and, oddly enough - just begging to have romance frolicking on its beach, where memories of "once was," - are "gone;" and, all that remains is the reminisce of dreams blown into the sands. The strength to survive the climate has overwhelming harmed you mere existence, for even "love," the undivided strength given by God in his holy name. Reluctantly you remain in the sea of life, pretending it doesn't bother you; standing tall and vigilant, reminding us all how you can make it – alone!

For it was once said, "No man is an island!" Did the writer mean male - or anybody? Not sure either, but applicable! I pray to God for your strength; but, not to the point of your independence. Although the beaches are so inviting, the ocean so warm and blue; there - even the pebbles on the beach get tossed and turned, drawn in the undertow by the ocean waves...... God bless you!

It's a Pretty Day for a Walk in the Shade

    The day was young, and an old friend invited me to come out to enjoy the sun with him. I walked few blocks down the street to go to where he said we'd meet. Everyone along the way - smiled at me as they- too enjoyed the day. "Oh, it's a pretty day for a walk in the shade!"

    I got to the bench that stood in the shade, waiting for me to take my place. As I waited for my friend to show, I noticed the sun was so nice and warm. My heart was filled with warmer thoughts too; of you, and I even thought, "I wish this day could last all year long." But – "Oh, it's a pretty day for a walk in the shade!"

    I reclined and stared at the fall colors on the leaves. "My," I thought – they're happy too as they danced together amongst themselves. The gentle breeze orchestrates!!! - I catch a glimpse of geese as they parade across the sky. "Yes! "They too enjoy the blue, a cloud, or two passes by. I hear them utter to themselves; "It's a pretty day to fly in the sky," as I walk along in the shade.

    I smile and look down; I wonder if my friend got side tracked along the way; got busy, or forgot, after all; it was he that invited me. The squirrels play as they gather before winter comes. I think, "I hope not! I hate the cold!" So I'll just sit here and wait; it's too pretty a day to hurry, and let it get away. The sun now shines upon my face. "Oh, it's a pretty day for a walk in the shade!

    I sat and thought, my dear friend, "Was he here; in spirit?" Just was taking care of other things, and just wanted me to stop along the way; find the sun, and enjoy the shade. I thought, "Yes, maybe - I was led away from my routine to capture this day that was made for me; to sit here on this bench, and pay tribute to the one who made this wonderful day; taking me out of the sun, for a walk in the shade.

Jessie's Dad

There in a cradle, a child is born; created by God so magnificently; healthy and well, perfectly in God's image; this tiny infant, a blessing in His sight - now sleeping. A baby who's future; undetermined, deserves more than a mom to take care of her! "But where is he as priorities dictate?" "Out to lunch? - - A meeting after dark! - - Certainly not in church, on Sunday morning!"

In her innocence; learning, and developing; ever mindful, her mentor is missing! Jessie listens as it's only her mother who has time to watch that little child as she turns into an adolescent. As she finds her own way; her first date; holding hands, a kiss maybe; little Jessie is all grown up! One day, her mom now gray, kisses her goodbye as she climbs on a bus; headed off to college; and in this great big world, that cute little girl will become another number, branded for life.

After the first semester, Jessie brings her boyfriend home, pregnant! There, the cycle of life starts all over again. Sadly, little Jessie's story is as customary, as father's relish enjoying the freedoms of prosperity without recourse of responsibility.

Today, I pray for all those little Jessie's that never had mentoring; homelessly searching for direction and, lost on Sunday morning; a glimmer of hope as God with open arms, surrounds their spirit - nurturing their empty heart.

Last Dance

After six months at sea, finally a leave; shore duty; dry land; a barrack; a bed - not a bunk; where being tossed, and turned, was the ship, not me - trying to sleep. Finally in! Laundry done; now it was time for me; enjoy a book I'd like to read. It was late May, the fragrance of spring remained. You'd never know a war was going on over there. Germany and France at odds; and - I'm ready for some peace and quiet!

The N.C.O. was throwing a memorial dance; of which, I had no intentions of going; but, the C.O. highly recommended, I attend. "Yes Sir, I'll go!" With an invitation like that - how could I say, "NO"? A few days away - some sun and R-n-R were mainly on my mind; wrote to my mom: "Hi, doing fine… "How's dad doing? – "You okay?" I needed to let them know I was in from sea.

Friday morn - I was up early laying out my dress whites for the night; still didn't feel like I needed to be present; just another face in the crowd - you know; but, I'm going nonetheless.

I arrived at 7:45 - - - the place was packed! I know why - the band was outstanding. Everybody came to dance, and see who'd they meet; but, as for me - I was more interested in just hanging out for romance wasn't in my cards – at least not as far as I could see. Oh, I danced a few with some I never knew; and, as the evening grew - the crowd began to thin. Standing out in the courtyard full of roses and tulips, was "YOU!" - Inquisitive, I came to see if you were okay - and with you head down and looking away - you said to me "I've waited all night to see if you noticed me. I gave up and came outside to smell the flowers, and enjoy the breeze. I said "Mam, my apologies." "What can I say" And as you turned, and looked up at me, "Say Sure," and "have the last dance with me"

So with the band playing something slow and soft, I forgot what it was - I was lost in the love I found that night. Dancing in the courtyard under the moonlight.

Life

    I walked back down to where we first meet; I thought about how intrigued I was with you! The laughs, and joy, such happiness that followed; my thoughts and memories surrounded by the months we played together. The summer winds and the evenings spent, playing on that merry-go-round. I'd run as fast as my little legs would travel to see how fast I could spin you. Then we'd stop and try to walk -- laughing at each other. We'd hold on to one another, praying the other wouldn't fall. We'd rest and sit a spell; listen to the waves breaking on the beach.

 But - that was then; and, two generations later, times have changed. We've not seen each other since then. Well it's been almost fifty years! Our parents played bridge as we enjoyed our little lives, playing together; riding our bikes, speeding up and down the hills, making forts in your back yard as we tried to hide from the rest of the world. I've thought of you a time or two as I have traveled hither and yond; but, now I thought, it was time to come back home. I wonder if you'll show. It's nothing like I remember! The grass has withered and the cabanas are in disrepair; but, sitting all alone is our little merry go round; frozen in time, where we first found love. Walking over to see if I could find where we took a rock and scratched out our names; the merry-go-round had rusted and didn't spin anymore.

 I sat with my coat tightly wrapped around me. The winter breeze gave an annoying chill that penetrated through me, waiting! Life for me, had full circled; and, all those many years away - didn't matter. Watching, I turned to look where I'd parked. I thought I heard a noise; must have been the wind. I guess I was only dreaming! It was a nice thought. I looked out over the river, rough, and cold; and, gray as winter reminded me of loves lost. I wished you'd showed; but, I was the only creature willing to bear the elements, praying. I walked back to sit in my car, trying desperately to get warm again; I closed my eyes and said, "Lord, where is this life that I prayed for…where memories keep me warm and love motivates our hearts… As I prayed - a peck sounded on the window. You showed, after all!!! "You gonna let me in, or am I just going to freeze out here?" I got out and walked you around to the other side, giving you a hug. I opened the door for you. Walking back, I thought, "Thank you, Lord!"

We spent an hour or so reminiscing over things. It was so nice to see you again; but, too many years had left us weary. We said goodbye. "May I drive you home?" "No, I'll walk"….. She opened the door. Disappointed I could see she too wanted more. I guess this is where memories part ways; and dreams are heavenly; where God is faith, and life is….temporary at best!

Mallards and Monkeys

Today in the rain, I thought it was time to call in sick; and, read my bible from cover to cover. "Guess what - l did?" "You know what?" "We are all doomed!" - Born from sin! We learn to lie before the truth is uttered; and, hate as children before we love. Then we bend the truth to suit our intentions; and, deceive if it's necessary, and of course - lust on occasion. So face it -- biblically speaking - none of us are going to make it - to that place they call heaven above...

And as it goes, I sit and wait on the right one to knock; but do I dare let her in - maybe or maybe not! You know, I think I've seen this screen play before!!! - But yes, the book teaches patience, and to wait on The Lord, for all good things come to those who do. And yes; I've had a brush with love a time or two; but, nothing compares to our fine feathered friends, or those who hang around - hoping to get noticed out there on the branch.

There lies no sin from within, and no conscience to decide if it's wrong or if it's right. - But united for life, the two swim across a pond - making waves; amongst themselves, for none other shall come between them. And, as they bare the elements of time - north and south; they endure what Mother Nature brings, protecting their vow.

And those primates deserve the same for they love, and have off spring; and, sin never enters in. I thought, how strange is it - for not the love of God that animals by design - respect, cherish, and honor; where us humans can't even decide. "What's up with that!!!?" I asked myself, "Why should we die for the sins that are placed within, long before we are born; animals don't have them. Okay, well, maybe a dog; but most of the wild kingdom doesn't; and yet, we are condemned. I don't get that either, I thought to myself!!!

I really loved once, and cherished that one too; and, for it not to be a sin; or, as it's removed - as though it never happened. So is sin the culprit? Today we just play according to its rules. I think.... - But it's our conscience that dictates the playing field (vow) - and is God merely the empire, trying to keep score! Maybe....

Marooned

There I woke like a bad dream, a storm...I guess. The palm fronds waking me from a dead sleep; trying to recover myself; and, I couldn't find my sheets. My eyes still closed, trying to find comfort as I thought, I lay in my bunk. The sunshine in one eye; and slowly, opened the other, trying to see what happened.

Stretched out on the sand; itching from sleeping on the beach, I raised my head, focusing. A half a mile away - my sailboat, in ruins lay horizontal on a reef. I thought to myself, "What the hell happened?!!!" I turned my head the other way; just as I thought - more sand. Raising myself up to my knees, trying to straighten my back, and scratching my head trying to recall the past few days... "I couldn't!!!" ....

I staggered to my feet, making sure I could walk; and, that nothing was broke; I looked around to see if anything else washed ashore. I started to walk; straining to listen to see if I could hear any noise. All I heard was the roar from the surf of the ocean; not even a shoe print appeared in the sand. "Pretty sure..... I was definitely "Marooned"....

Walking around the island, scattered with debris; I saw what looked like pages, flapping in the wind, off in the distance; half buried on the beach and not in any hurry. I moseyed along, dragging my feet. I thought about my wife and kids, I left at home. I had no way to contact them! "My phone!" I'm sure it was lost overboard; sailing in the tropics, a long lost dream. I guess it might as well have been on my bucket list for all it means! I, "marooned," stuck - - my boat in ruins; and.... well..... I guess this is it!!! ---- "No food" "no water" .....

Casually I strolled down the beach, looking out; the ocean looked like a post card, or a great jigsaw puzzle. Here I was, nonetheless, combing the beach looking for treasure. Lo and behold, weathered in the sand, a particle part of a book - buried beneath. I stopped and picked it up to see what it said; dusted it off, and on the top of the page, it read, "Genesis." Great I said, just what I needed to read.

I hung my head...turned; and, sat on the sand and thought, "Okay, God," "How are you going to get me out of this one? "No phone" "No food" "No water" - - - "Marooned!!!" "Lord, help me - I think.... I'm doomed!" ....

I started to cry reading the weathered words of God. I could only think of my family and my predestination to a charted isle, unfulfilled. But there, my tears fell like rain, searching my soul, my faults and guilt before me; I thought, God has humbled me now - to nothing. I stood up, bowed my head; and, said "Lord you're amazing!" "How you can take me from material and wealth, to nothing in the darkness of just one night!" I dusted off the back of my shorts from where I sat and started on my journey, walking again, searching for an answer that might help me out of this desolation...

I walked around a point where the sand and palms, merged in beauty. I thought, "Why am I here?" Huge boulders that look to be planted in position were a sight to behold! I walked around one and past another; and, a voice spoke, "Where you going in such a hurry?" Startled - I looked; and, just like out of a story book, "My Lord!" I said.

"Why am I here in this desolate place?" "Please I pray, take me home to my family where I belong!" "Not so fast," He returned. "You must believe in me and my Father." I again hung my head, and fell to my knees weeping. "Please forgive me!" I begged..... I looked up, the Lord was gone. Alone and desolate; but faith - the faith that all hope wasn't gone. Clenching the pages of Genesis again I prayed.
"Father, let your will prevail".

And then it dawned, I'm not alone for God knows my situation or He wouldn't have sent His son. Comforting as it was, some coffee and a bite to eat would sure help as well; but, there was none. "No food! No water! Now fasting!

I watched the moon rise twice from a bed of palm fronds lying in the sand, the stars so bright they really did twinkle. I laughed and thought to myself, recollecting what happened the day before. I asked God to please save me from paradise of hell. "I will repent and straighten up and take my family to a church of their liking." "I pray dear Lord as I fall off to sleep, to protect me; and, bless my family… for they are all I have!"

The following day, I woke and went to the boat; raised a sail in case they were searching; and, looked for something that wasn't stale; looked for my phone and couldn't find it. I went back to the beach to read again sitting in the sand - my toes in the water; and, with what's left of my tattered bible, I prayed!

And as I read, I heard something. The rumble of an engine, then a voice, "Honey - you OK?" I jumped to my feet and waved my shirt; there - on the bow of an old fishing trawler, stood my wife. I yelled, "What are you doing out here?" She yelled "I had planned to surprise you when you got into port and sail home with you while mom kept the kids." I bowed my head and said, "Thank you Father! I know it was you that brought her here; and, in my time of need!" "I'll honor my promise – Lord!" "You'll see!"

The following Sunday I went back to where we were married; and, I stood before the congregation and told them the story. There unbeknownst to me, sat a publisher who after service came and said, "Write your story, and I'll help you share your recollections."

So between fighting with insurance companies and writing my novel, I took six weeks off, and every Sunday I did what I promised..... Thanks be to God for this second chance!!!

Maybe Later

I thought about you as I sat in my pew, alone with only my faith trying to protect what's left of me. Every Sunday, we are taught that our dear Lord is here for us for there in the pages; "biblically speaking," are filled with the promises of a "another coming" with our expectations reinforced Sunday to Sunday; We wait!!! Alone - I sit - for prayers are spoken; and, promises are broken as disappointments follow from day to day, month after month.

I try to believe that God has a plan but the only words that come to mind, are "maybe later!" I guess maybe I see how Jesus felt as he went about His life trying to persuade; and, there I too try to let you see the way; a life with harmony and joy, shared ---should be; and, as I wait on dreams to come, " maybe later " is still the only response.

The clouds of thunder rumble in the distance, the earth prepares to receive the rain, and love is quenched; but there I remain, reminded of the cracked desert earth, starving for water, where life has died from starvation. "Maybe later," it shall rain and the blessings promised will be answered. But, still alone I sit, watching as the world turns feeling forgotten; remembering, "Maybe later!" Then a touch on my shoulder; I turned but there's no one there! I listen to hear -- is there a voice that sheds a little light on, still in the spirit - I pray; but there, the answer then comes…"Maybe later." I turn the page; "the grass withers, the flower fades; but, the word of God will stand forever!

Patiently, I listen to the hopes and dreams as we sit separately waiting; but, maybe later prayers will be answered. As Satan enjoys shredding love that comes by God, I watched.... I listened.... I wondered..... "Maybe later!"

Melting

Finally, I thought I'd met the one who'd captured my heart, lit up my spirit, and; "Yes," swept me of my old feet as well. I thought about you as I labored in the summer heat, how refreshing it is to be in your arms. I thought about the memories we could make together; the love, the intimacy, the warmth of our hearts being next to one another; but, it wasn't even lunch, and trying to focus on what I was supposed to be doing was only going to get worse as day lingered on.

The heat from the sun of the past few days had taken its toll; and, being soaking wet from sweat at nine a.m., gave me little hope of melting into you as the evening comes. Dead -- drained of stamina; my thoughts of melting into you, kept me going as I looked at the clock now nine fifteen.

But -- Refreshed from the shower as the water seeped into my bones; I thought, "God how wonderful it was to stand here, and melt away as the shower cleansed what was left of my body; and, then to feel the towel as you dried me like a massage after a trip across the Mojave desert." I turned to face the love that blanketed me, and melted into your heavenly arms.

Yes, I guess I was only dreaming; but, nonetheless - it is there where the melting pot is stirred; and, as I thought intimately, love would follow. I know there's not many times in life where your heart's ignited on fire, casting your feelings - like sitting on a dock, fishing as your feet dangle in the water while waiting on the 'big one' to take the bait. As

I lay there counting the revolutions of the ceiling fan, I can't help but wish you were next to me sharing in the cool breeze created with love as we entangle ourselves, melting into each other arms. I hug my pillow! ...

As I drift off to where the waters kiss the shore; I pray, Lord - let the day come where I too melt away in your spirit; and, find that holy love that comes only once in a lifetime; and, may I be blessed by You! ....

Memories

After these many months, it was time - I thought, to take you home to the place where I was reared; its' a pretty place - the foliage and trees, the boats, beach, and salt water. The history and the legacies; the landmarks, and the hand-made brick alley ways; but, in that tiny port of tall ships, once the capitol of those thirteen colonies; I'd walk you along the cobblestone, and take snapshots of you standing beside those landmarks, and monuments. I'd take you back in time; the history, and build a scrap book of new memories!

I'd like to show you where I learned to kiss my first love, and where we took long walks through the woods, sat upon the ivy wall, and smelled the honeysuckle as it's fragrance dominated the atmosphere; and, show you the homes where we moved into, and yet they've changed as the memories remain; though it was yesterday, and you and me were back in high school.

Oh, those fond memories I'd love to have shared with you as memory lane would have had your name on every street post! I would have loved that! We'd sail across to the other side and kiss, out of my mother's watchful eye. We'd fill the boat with dreams, and watch them come true as we sailed away; off into the summer sunset.

Yes, the things I want to share with you…. - since it wasn't you I grew up with; but, to stroll down memory lane to where my parent's home once was, would fill my heart and make it smile; to have you there, holding your hand; and, sharing. To remember when --- with you my love!!!

Missions

    Traveling through space at supersonic speeds; light years away from heaven, I'm on a mission! God has commanded me to go out and fulfill a dream; touch a heart, maybe make a smile! Starring into the space above; heaven is out here "somewhere," but at this rate, I could miss it as I'm traveling way too fast ---
"There - the gates!!!," I yelled. I just passed 'em!!!! Maybe, I'm to stop in on my return trip from "where-ever" I'm being sent.

So this is my mission! - To journey out to where faith is a road map. "Should I pack a bag?" Will I be gone long?" - I wonder where I'm going; I wonder where "is" this place God has intended for me? "Where!" - Where life is the beauty of living, and hopefully with God as my pilot; I will succeed, and reach the level where I'm supposed to conquer.

"Yes!" Short of stopping to refill for fuel; it's a million miles an hour just to reach the other side; "Of where?" "I'm not quite sure; but, believing is all that's asked, and trust is the engine that keeps us running as we are trying to reach for the stars."
"God's call'n," "I'm off! I have an appointment on the 25th hour of the day after tomorrow; to stand before the creator. This is going to be interesting, I thought!

    Now, I'm traveling at the speed of light; sitting back, watching the stars as they go by - so fast! "What's the hurry?" "Why am I rushing through life; just to have it over?" "I thought to myself," I need to slow down…"But it's too late! - I've been called; and, well - you know, I think - I ought not be late!" ….

    Standing in a completely white room where walls, floors - ceiling too, are all the exact same color white; but, one wall was solid glass, and the view…spectacular, I guess it's where God watches you. It's me this time… looking out over the Garden of Eden. I ponder trying to comprehend; the flowers are like none you can imagine; purple, blue, yellow, and pink and orange; but oddly no red at all! "Hmmmm, I thought!" "Why, I wonder. God only sheds His grace, waiting with anticipation; a voice, "sit down!"

"Where?" "Anywhere" ……But, there are no chairs!
    "Sit! - I command." "There's nothing there!" I sat…"Wow!" There is a chair under me! How'd that happen? "Oh!" I forgot where I was. It was white - and matching; silently, I poised. "Relax, I heard." I thought, "That's a little hard to do after a million-mile journey and a meeting with God." With nerves of metal I said, "What did I do?" "Nothing?" "Pardon the pun….Oh my God!!!" "What did I do to be called before your presence?" I have chosen you to go out, and be an example of my love. I thought before I answered, "Is this a trick question or something?" Ok my dear Lord, how do I do that?

"Bring peace to the world?" I paused and thought about my answers. After a few -I said, "Where do I start?" In the light of the white…God spoke, "You need to commence," "Oh! This is bizarre, bring peace - commence – "What?" …"How? And with that, I was off in a supersonic flight back to earth. All I could think about was "How do I deliver what I've been requested?" Feeling like I was free falling in an elevator from the nine hundredth floor, all I could think about is what I'm supposed to do once it stops.

Then gradually my flight slowed, then it stopped and doors opened. I stepped out ---- I wasn't home.

I looked toward the heavens, "Are you kidding me? I thought, "This isn't funny! "Start," was all He said. "I looked all around after my feet hit the ground again, and then it dawned .... "Who's going to believe this story?" "Who's going to believe my mission?" "Nobody - That's who!!! I then realized it wasn't a mission at all; but, a test of strength to see if I could endure. That's what I thought! "Does anyone here speak English?"

Then as He instructed, I was faced with an altercation of where love and peace, were the only answer. Still I asked, "Why me?" I stood in middle of what could be a Holocaust! I prayed! No one spoke my words; but, they all knew as I prayed, what my message was; as "love" was spread - no matter the faith. Love is stronger than any language. Quickly as I looked up, I was home - back on familiar turf. Today, I look at where I was… I ask "Was it my mission in life?" "I search .... "What is yours?"...

Back on earth…..

More Wax

At 6:04 I rolled out, filled up my truck, ran to the bank - get ready for work; have a cup of coffee, grab a hard-boiled egg, and head off - Running late! It's hump day - half way there, another one in the history books; taking the scenic way for a change, avoiding the hum-drum traffic; giving myself a chance to think, I really thought about the vicious cycle most of us live.

A roulette wheel - if you will. Whether you play black or red - you'll probably loose. Where deals are made in the dark of night, and deadlines are met with seconds flat…the computer world, where you can invest after 5 overseas; and, make a return by morn while others sleep.

We are burning the candle at both ends of the stick, hoping we don't get caught trying to juggle finances and kids… life in the fast lane! I'm glad I took the scenic way.... Yes, and then, there's the stress that comes along with it as our demands outweigh the needs; but, we aren't satisfied as we live in a plastic house; rolling the dice, and figuring out which bills to pay come Friday.

"Oh Lord, will ever end - the roller coaster that never stops; or, the merry-go-round that never quits." As you go to church, and pray; we ask – "What's the benefits, if we can't believe that our purpose; there it's nothing more, than to cycle through a generation…Boy, that's beneficial!"

Maybe it's time to stop pretending, and when you go the doctor next time; feeling ill and stressed; and, he looks at you - says your fine---- Nothing that a little "more wax" won't fix !!!

Morning

  There with you, I lay; my mind, a million miles an hour; clammy - my body needed you. I wanted so much to touch the miracle God had brought into my life. I smelled your fragrance; the aroma of love that kept pouring out from the night before. I turned to hold the mirage that lay beside me - if only for a minute; the love that has encapsulated me has grown to heights above the heavens. But, a soft peaceful smile - as your hands turned, and tucked up under your pillow.

 I watched you… it seemed for hours; I listened to you exhale, over and over. I wondered what you were dreaming; or, was your mind finally at rest - the end of a journey that led you to me… Imagining the yellow brick road had finally brought you home… I am so happy! Only God can perform miracles; and, it was finally my turn. I lay there, and stared at your features.

Your brow resembled the soft sands that build the dunes; your nose, the slopes of newly fallen snow; your lips, a dessert a gourmet cook prepared for me to put mine on; and, your jaw line, your chin - sculptured by a famous artist in the fifteenth century; the lines created by His holy Majesty! My eyes could not imagine that God knew exactly what I wanted!

  Joy and solitude, the place where intimate peace; God allows love to be expressed by even tiny little things - even while you're asleep. I watched……. So in love ……not even having to touch…the peaceful expression said it all! A twitch as you opened just an eye, a smile, "What are you doing?" faintly you said. "Staring at you - I replied!" "And why?" she said. I proceeded, "I don't know why; but, God has given me this gift to share, my body is in awe over you -- a goddess under my covers!!! ---- I'm so lucky to be in love."

Mothers

Today as I sit where I so often do, listening; my thoughts reflecting. But, it's the ones alive, I know so well - that God has blessed them with the gift - that only comes from a child. And as I write, my mom - is there in spirit; for she lost her happiness in '81, and my brothers and me - live in memory, now only.

And –so, its "those children," that I address to be blessed with the one that gave them life; they should commemorate it every day; but, they do not - so we set aside a beautiful Sunday in May, when we proudly walk along together to thank our Lord for our moms.... For their mothers days are numbered… to celebrate the honor, the love - the perseverance; to put up with us, as we explore our own lives. They gave us all they could to make our happiness – even happier in our life.

So my children, never ever forget your creator, forgive them for their faults as I did. They're only human; and, none-the-less, they're your mother! Please realize today in your supersonic life to take the day; stop, and give remembrance to them ... If it's only for a day!

And, may the Lord above - remember you, as you take time to spend some time loving them………….your mom!!!----- Amen....

My Carol

Tis the season; well, its' close…and, as it approaches; the word - of course, that comes to me, "Rejoice!" - For its' a perfect time to thank the lord above, for His many blessings. I think of friends I've met throughout this year - some were just acquaintances; but, some are so dear…and, it's those I chose to thank God for!

Today I thought, "I want to sing - for my harmony in life has come --caroling." The joy I have received from you this years' past, is immeasurable; the sounds of holidays sustain my heart; for I sit with my friend, and love what this day brings.

People smiling and singing their favorite carol, trying to stay in harmony for they sing from their heart as I see - their life is good; and, God has blessed where they are. The colors are so bright; and, illuminate the sky - and even the stars shine down upon us as we carol through the night. "What child is this - that has brought us life; and, demands us to give thanks to God?" – "For He shed His grace; that we may be blessed to be alive, and rejoice in His company."

It's my carol that I want you to hear… not in your ear; but, in your heart - for I sing of things that have brought this year to a close. Rejoicing, thanking our Dear Lord, for everything; and, for those who have lost - trying to sing… "Rejoice! For those gone – are now on high."

And as the day draws near; gifts are bought, the tree is lit. It's time to share the cheer, Egg Nog…for it warms the hearts. God knows! We smile - commemorate another year.

Praise Be to God! For these words - I carol with you; our hearts in harmony, our smiles in symmetry; and, our love --never to part.

As one goes by - and we ring in a new; we look forward to another "carol," we may sing together for the rest of our

My Last Day

So today I realized, "This was it!" The love I prayed for had come and gone. My life, worth nothing - was over! My day's number was up! I woke and made my bed - heaven forbid - it not be made! Did the dishes, and straightened the house. I didn't want anyone to find me in a disheveled house. I wrote you a love letter, just in case I left early. But the fact remained, things were over! I thought to myself… what if I don't go to heaven, then where would I be? "Alone!" "Oh, I've been there already." I knew how that was going to feel! Preparing for the inevitable, certain things didn't matter anymore. Giving up, I thought about you; what I prayed for that never came true. Searching my soul, and asking our Lord, "Why?" "What happened, like it really mattered now!" Knowing my life was over, I was leaving for destinations, untold. I gave up on the love I wanted. It didn't really want me, and I was ready to throw in the towel. Who cared! Not you, nor our children. I felt as if I was just in the way; corrupting things, and making it worse. Pull the plug! To "hell" with it! I wouldn't be missed a bit.

I sat, waiting on my last breath. I didn't care! Death would be a welcomed relief, I thought to myself. My heart aches and the pain would at least, be gone; even if my tired broken body remained. I didn't care! In my favorite chair I waited; not in any pain particularly; but, waiting just the same. A knock came upon my door. "Do I dare answer?" "Why," I thought… "Nothing matters!" "I'm down to hours now." Another knock! "Oh, My Lord; who could it be?" "Jesus!" "It's you, I exclaimed!!!" "May I come in?" "Of course…of course; I replied!!!" "Please, sit!" "A glass of water?" "Thanks, I don't have time." I know those words, I thought as it came to be. "Your life is mine, and only I will tell you when its time!" "Change your course; let the wind fill your sails!" He said. "What does that mean, I wondered"....

I fell asleep where He left me. I woke the next the morning, rested of all things; and, refreshed, ready to conquer whatever life had left for me. Reflecting, I thought about my past, now gone from view; or, at least in my mind. Nothing but the future! The past released, like it never happened; and then, God spoke..... "Go in peace as I let love last forever!"...... Mesmerized in disbelief, I got up…nothing hurt; not even my glasses made it worse! My normal aches were no more. Had I died? .... I didn't know; just nothing hurt anymore! My phone rang, it was you! "Good morning; and, how are you feeling?" I thought… "What a strange way to ask!" I said, "If I told you all that's happened in the last twelve hours you couldn't!!!" I had come prepared to leave; but, I was informed by Jesus himself as He came knocking on my door… reminding me it's only He that has the power to say "when." I woke again and nothing hurt. I put on my glasses and they made it worse. It's like I had been reset to when I was four. I can't hardly believe; a miracle of sorts. I remember nothing of my past. Guess I'm not supposed to - as I recollected to you.

I went to church the next morn. I sat where I always do; with the same group I've come to know. As the sermon was being read, I could quote the message out of my head. Now this was "unimaginable," I've never read the scripture, ever! The next passage came, and I knew it as well! Not wanting to alarm anyone, I just followed along through the service; but, after I caught up with Brother Bob, and told him the story; he looked at me and said, "Son you've been – Touched!" I said, "Sir, I think I have; for Jesus came and sat on my couch the night before. Pastor looked at me; smiled and said, "I could tell!" Puzzled how; I asked. "I watched you read your bible from the balcony without your glasses!"

My Walk

I went for a walk just to see where it goes, but the path was winding, and long; and as I walked along the flowers, their fragrance was strong; but, camouflaged among their beauty were stickers and thorns.

The gentle rolling hills covered in green grain, gave way to mountains that sculptured the heavens; and, as I climbed my way thru life; even the sky as rich, and blue - had clouds of thunder; but, they too showed promise with their silver lining.

Up on a ledge I stopped and purged. I asked God, "Is this the way…Are you sure?" As He spoke; He said, "I led you out of a pit-of-hell from things you knew not; for I have opened the gate to give you - life as you pursue. "Do not stop, for I am the way!" I turned to look back; my fragrant path was all but gone! Life has "no reverse," I thought; so, I have no choice but to travel on. I climbed to the crest of the peak to see what I could see and there before me, "Utopia" waiting on me. I smiled, and chuckled to myself!

"I had missed it," I thought, yet all along that little word, laid hidden - top, and all this time I walked in the valleys. I see now that God had saved the best for last! He gave his grace for me where I may inherit the only thing I cannot buy; for I submit myself to…"Thine."
My soul, my spirit, my body --- I am free!!! And….there, I cry…….

Nature's Dignity

There in the cool morning dew, I sat on my lani and listen to a whippoorwill as he was trying to find anyone to talk to. Quietly, I sipped my coffee so as not to disturb him. In the morning twilight, an owl answered him back. Smiling to myself, I listened....... A moment of silence; and, then the whippoorwill responded to the owl obliviously answering him.

Now so often we wonder; do birds of other denominations converse with one another? Then the owl replied. Smiling I thought; is this a Kodak moment, or what; if it just wasn't so dark. Then I thought, "How wonderful it was to watch God's creatures in the natural." I sipped my coffee, and looking down, I wondered why us humans have to destroy our own. How ungodly are we! We leave church, get into our cars; and, it's every man for 'himself!' Or, we go to another land; and, we have to sleep with one eye open, trying to protect ourselves; and then, there in the early light - these two converse like there old buddies ....

Preposterous! Two birds have more respect than some that are raised with common sense. In retrospect as I got another cup, knowing I needed to get under way; I bid my new buddies a farewell, and thought, "Hopefully…will enjoy your company tomorrow." And there I was, blessed to know that not just man; but, birds as well, have dignity for one another. What a pleasant thought to go work with…..Be blessed!......

Never Enough

Traveling back from five days of hard labor - I had time to collect my thoughts, as two words spun around in my head, "never enough," ...absolutely not – satisfied! Two words I wonder, should we ever put together. I watched as children try to please their parents; and, parents constantly trying to earn their children's love. How sad it was, they're both so obviously trying to make a difference, and neither is content with others' desires.

Examining the trust of where love begins, I witnessed hurt evolving from efforts where both are trying; but, never relinquishing their power for control of situations, manifests its self almost back to slavery times! Then I thought, "Lord Have Mercy," and, after I made that comment, I looked at myself and laughed. Ha there's where "never enough" comes into play. Prayer!!! For only the love of our dear Lord, do we seek would "never enough" be a commitment ... And as those dissatisfied in life have come to a place of "never enough," I ask myself,

"Will they ever be happy?" "Probably not; for so many - not enough money, or never enough time, need new clothes, or a bigger home." The adrenalin rush that's created only confirms that - only God - is where "never enough" is lacking. I asked myself, "Do I have wants? Sure, but it's not a power struggle of desire, merely a simple prayer that I be blessed and let The Almighty do the rest; for the power of prayer is much stronger than the absence of our father and we often take control when things don't go our way.

Yes "never enough," sadly stated - shows just how unhappy some people are; and, if they would apply the phrase to the power of God; the gifts would fall from heaven like rain - if we all would just give it a "try to" again! Prayer! Amen....

Never Knew

"I just thought I'd stop to write you; but, I just knew you were goin' out with someone new." I got on a ship yesterday morn – deployed to a land I've never been before; but, I'm sure you won't wait on me as I travel overseas.

I'm really sorry I won't be home on Christmas eve; Uncle Sam has bigger plans for me; even though I wish I could be under your tree to open on Christmas morn.
And as I stand out on the deck on New Year's eve, I know you're on the dance floor where you met me; but, now He's new - and it's not me you're with - to celebrate.

I'll miss you and our love we shared. The two of us were great; but, just not good enough for you to save yourself for me – 'cause you're gone to find another, where I used to be.

My duty is done, I'm comin' home. I wonder if you're home alone; or, married with a baby born, or back in school, or workin' hard, and waiting on me. I don't know, but I hope so!

It's Friday night - I got to know what you're up to! I can't wait to see! "Are you home alone?" - And as I knock, a baby cries. In your arms - you open the door to greet me in; and you say to me; "The baby's ours!" I've sat home alone, waiting and hoping you were coming back to me. So let's go back to the dance floor where it all began. I'll find a sitter, and we'll get out of here… back to where we were before you were deployed!!!

No Regrets

    And then as I rolled to face you, I caressed your breast, and kissed you on your shoulder blade; holding on to you as if it was going to be our last; I licked your neck as I lay beside you. "Don't move, I'll bring you a cup of coffee." Getting up, I felt uneasy but I thought it must just be me. We lie there sharing the early morn, watching an old black and white over coffee as the sun came peeking through the pane.

    Kissing you at the door to say goodbye; you stood clothed in your serenity, smiling - never thought it would be our last; but as you waved, and closed the door - somehow I could tell what it really meant. I drove off, staring at the windows. Maybe I'd see you wave; but, there was nothing - not even a peek. Oh, I thought I was imagining things; it's all in my head, I said to myself, "Certainly not - this wasn't the end!

  So on a gorgeous morning, I went to worship, seeking answers - I knew not; for only God could enlighten me. I prayed, "Lord help me!" "Show me what you want for me; let me be a servant for You." "I pray, Lord for unanswered - answers..."

For all those many confusing months, I cried at home – alone; waiting on you to come - commit to one; but, there I was - not good enough. You played your game, and destroyed my broken heart. There as time had passed, I gave you everything; my heart, my soul - even my body couldn't satisfy you; determined to hurt, I grew distant from the pain. Yet I remained, hoping, praying, asking God for guidance!

 As we all pray for miracles, not even twenty four hours had passed; "No regrets! My Lord let me receive a message that clearly, without question - the best for my salvation. I turned, and walked away..... May I go, and grow - for the Lord has saved me! No more hurt, no more maybe later, no regrets!!! It's over!

Our Crowns

    And here in the misty dawn, I sit on my couch, and stare out. I wonder where you've gone, praying there - the day will come you'll realize what you've done. But even still, I stare – praying! I thought about the "crown of thorns," we all must bear as we endure our own - crucifixion. And I look out over the meadows to where we all want to be; saved by His grace. But there starring out my little window, praying for your return as God too wants you as one of his chosen; - in your time of desperation, I want the same.

    Yes, I see and even feel the crown of thorns for you; but, as it pertains to me? And the deeper I thought of my brothers' love, we all carry our crosses to bear - for only God can save us from the crowns we dawn. There in the morning mist, it's you I see - donning a crown of thorns as you too have crosses to bear. Can a crucifixion be far ahead - created by our misgivings?

    But it's only God who can save us! Obey His command (Nehemiah 1:5). We live here, we are in the ways of the world; we can't distain right from wrong. Sadly we give ourselves; but, not for His mercy. We live alone, determined to fill our voids of joy - monetarily trusting; and, there - the meek shall inherit the earth.

    And there on my couch the fragrance remains, but your love has gone; for other thoughts, commands, astray where you are. Even God cannot stop you; a blind eye cannot see, for the road to recovery is not the one you're on; and, as the road of roses delicately hides the forbidden curves; it's the "crown of thorns" that bears the mark where we have made - a wrong turn.

    So my brothers' in love; I pray! Beware - for only in Christ Jesus shall we find happiness; and there on the couch, I stare – praying the fragrances you bear; you will be saved… and your "crown of thorns" - tossed to the winds in God's holy name! -- Amen.

Peace

There in the morning, long before dawn; my mind's awake, and thinking of you. I tossed and turned, stuck one leg out from under covers trying to cool my body down a little - it doesn't help.... I fluffed the pillow, and repositioned my head - desperately trying to get you out of my thoughts; but, it was no use; you weren't going anywhere. I lay in bed, and asked, "Lord what's the purpose in my thoughts to be caught up in a life that's not going anywhere?"

Then it dawned - the Lord said, "Good Morning," I heard Him as clear as any bell - told. Hearing my thoughts, I'm sure, -- I said, "Lord why am on this road - I'm on; haven't I seen this all once or twice before?" And, He laughed at me! - Lost, perplexed, I thought - what are you trying to tell me, your majesty? ..... Then,…...Nothing! .... "Where'd you go?" Is that all there is, I thought as I sat listening.

Looking out my window as the morning light began to shine; a cloud with a silver lining shone, lightning shooting out in every direction, I watched.... And then He said, "You travel like a cloud with all the beauty and strength one can have, not even creating a bit of thunder like the lightning you're watching; you're in such turmoil... There I sat, humbled by the similarity, troubled by His example. I asked, "And?".... "Find peace! He replied"....

I got up to turn a light on, as dawn was still too early. I opened the book, "Proverbs 16: 15, 16, 17." There was the answer! My coffee cold - my body trembled. I knew that life was nearly at the end; and, only God would renew that which was ruined. I paused, not wanting to move. I thought, "From there in the heavens the Lord spoke to me as I awoke." - Reaching out to grab me as I am falling. I looked, tumbling; and, there below a cloud - a cloud with a silver lining....

And as my fall now broken, I rest on my pillow where my head, filled with emotions..... for our dear Lord took a moment for me, to bring me to see as my heart has broken.
"Peace" is the only answer where joy will mend the weary."

Pillow Talk

    Flying over the Indian Ocean, the sun is gone; and, a shade of green precedes the dark. A weeklong trip, businesses of course has lead me away from things with you - I look forward to: Coffee in bed, an occasional "Hi" through the day; and, at thirty seven thousand feet above the earth, I recline my seat, get a blanket, and lay my head, dreaming of where last night with you we shared our "pillow talk" time together before we said good night and drifted off.

Of all the things our busy schedules have never interrupted, was our time to share our thoughts before we said our prayers. But now at these heights without you here, this eight-by-twelve little pillow is gonna have to do. More often than not we'd gaze into each other's hearts and feel the rhythm of our love as it now was Gods turn to bless us with a holy night; but not for the next week or so while I'm away.

  You're going to have to stand guard over our pillow time and save it till I get home again. I love our pillow talks, as intimate as they sometimes are, relaxing - we've met again from places afar, to hold; and kiss, and stare a while. I'll miss those moments most of all; for I kissed you goodbye long before dawn, and headed off to Indonesia for a little shopping spree, Sam sent me on.

    And here in the stars at thirty seven thousand feet, I said my prayers, asking God to bring me back - safe and sound to you my love - that lies down there on the other pillow. The love of my life, we share very little; but, our "pillow talks," some days are all we have between jobs and after school activities. I just love to snuggle with you, and wrap my leg and blanket over you; hold you tight, and say good-night drifting off to Neverland.

For only God sends angels to watch over us, and sprinkle sand from a beach somewhere off in that part of land; where dreams are made, and streets of gold. There we are, holding hands sleeping by the ocean. A new day awaits, for God has made, and gives to us - the gift to give to one another again. It's just such a comfortable feeling, knowing our love has grown, just because of our "pillow talk time".....

Rainy Day Decisions

It once was said "You can't shoot if you don't aim;" and, I replied - "nothing beats a trial but a failure." So who's right, me or the other guy? And there in the midst of trying to make a decision, the leaves keep falling and you have no choice: .... rake or bag 'em.... For as life drops those challenges upon our hearts, we too have a choice - to except or reject what God hands us. But if you reject, the next word in Webster's is "rejoice." Where, if we sit and reject the obvious, we become stagnant; and, life as you know it --- passes you by.

Sadly as I sit where rituals are performed, waiting on a miracle from heaven; and, the heavens thunder...... "Is today the day?" Maybe! I sit and wonder; can our dear father on this day we celebrate, bring relief as the rain soothes a drought? I pray the heavens will open and flood the earth with angels, answering our prayers. Standing in the rain and not getting wet, protected by faith - from drowning in the tears that left us here -- alone.... I listen to the thunder and wonder.

Yet God knows as lightning comes and sparks our spirit; that which once was… again, our souls are born once more in love, and comfort - trying to mend from the past. Yes, I see what God has tried to repair; the damaged hearts' of recollection. Looking back brings no satisfaction to our spirit; and, there in the quietness --- Faith comes from heaven, a guardian angel… she returns to earth. The thunder stops, the rain restrains - the clouds break; the blue shines on you like an eye of a hurricane. I pause, I pray, "God loves you!" "You'll be okay --- just as soon as the storm passes!" But it's there - we all must weather the falling leaves as the season changes....

And in the falling rain, I wait for you like a second coming.... praying God hears my thoughts through the thunder. "I love you; but, rain dilutes the promises we shared when we were younger; and, all that's left is --- the illusions of dreams, washed away in the rain from hurt where broken hearts lie dying."

Recollect

Tonight in the quiet, I listened as the air filtering through were you once sat; and as I recollect a million years ago, I miss the life you brought to me; even if it was - last Sunday! I turn and looked at your beauty and the grace that accompanied. I smiled as God looked down to see the joy where loneliness once was. I praised those moments as though they were hours for only He knew the void and the desires of my spirit.

There beside me, sat a blessing from God. Only He in his magnificent timing could have seen the quandary I had endured; and, by His strength, I eat, work, and sleep. My dream that came from the gift of love He bestowed on me for only with God's help may I succeed! Now, I know I am blessed as our dear Lord as brought me help! .....

My father in heaven, I must honor for He believes in me. He glorifies me as I magnify His name. Through our trials and tribulations, He keeps a hand on my shoulder, comforting! Anointed, I strive to give, and here, God has brought another of His gifts to me - "You!" I am so humbled!

You're so beautiful, right "to my right," for I could not have painted a picture where God knew what I needed, any better. Oh my Lord where blessings flow, I could not ever thank You enough for the love You have for me ....

Second Thoughts

Where were you when you stopped in your place; and, gave yourself the time to face the fact that; "What you thought, was it right;" or, "was it wrong?" So all day long it haunts you, "Was I right," or, "Maybe - I was not." We go along in life trying, wishing, praying - we are right. Still I sit, and can't help but wonder now that life is almost gone, my second thoughts are yelling.

I wonder if this road is the way to go, "Do I go left…is that right; or, is it right that I left the way that seemed to show that I was wrong. My second thoughts are all I have, you know; my first thoughts, well they went - out the window, I guess.

So, I persist - this quest of finding out if what I thought was I right, or not – it's apparent. That life's road I travel on; has too many streets that I desire. Never thought which way was right. Oh now my second thoughts encompass me, circling like a carousel with lights and whistles screaming.

 Oh my God help!!!! I can't believe I have traveled this far alone wandering; my second thoughts now puzzling me.

Senseless

So many times I have trusted in you; but, sadly I have been left to fend with the end of where life was supposed to begin. Never able to see where life took a wrong turn, and the dust blurred my vision - and it does. "Where is the love you promised?"- "Where is the commitment that was intended?" Still, I measure the worth of the love by the sadness in my heart as I see you near me; but, "Where is your heart?" "Somewhere else - I guess."

So today I pick myself up, and try start over, again - hoping this time might be right as we find ourselves struggling to find security as the fragile thing called "love" has been broken; and, for no reason. Should we be here together again; but alone, living in the fear of loneliness that creeps in our souls?

God, I don't understand the logic of what has happened, for price of sin is far too inexpensive; and, cheap as it is the costs that are unbearable. I sit and measure time between the pains that creep in me as I wonder why I sit here - allowing this hurt called "love" to be devoured.

Tomorrow is a new one, but is this - the end or the beginning; for as history repeats itself…. I wonder! I just can't help to think the thoughts that cause the pain I endure within.

God bless this situation as Satan has crawled into this relationship - again!!!

Serenity on the Severn

It's an unusually cool day for June; the clouds have given us an awesome blanket to shade us from the oppressive heat. I spent the afternoon straightening up from the past week. Watching the rain and listening to thunder, as it drowns out the dryer.... But none-the-less, I had my honey-do-list of things that I needed to do. I caught myself in a little "déjà vu," thinking about my mom and dad. I sat and looked at the pictures I took outside their home where I grew up - on the Severn.

Catching crabs with my best friend, Kirk; we'd bring home a bushel basket by 1:00, just from off the pier; and, from off the poles where it stood. Our parents loved us!!! Those were the days; but, that was a half a century ago - when we were young; and found ways to entertain ourselves besides watching the "Howdy Doody" show....

Yes, I looked at the old pier as it stands majestically over the water; where "serenity" comes to mind, as those peaceful memories remain. The stories that ole' pier could tell! The history it could share. Amazingly held captive at the water's edge; it's there that God blessed the love where my childhood remains. I am blessed to look back a half a century ago, and nothing had changed – it's just as I left it.

Now as my years are mostly over, I return -- in thought -- to share my new love with the memories of my roots! Oh Lord - the love I have for the heritage I share with her --- incomparable - A history book by itself; my recollections of events of many, many years - to pass on to the children.

Most of all, its mom and dad; I pray for them while they sit with you. I could never show the appreciation that's lead me back to where my little life started; and today, I want to share what God has done ....allowed me to take part of. "I love you more than you will ever know." For I bring gifts as God would request - of us all to share the love; and, the harmony of life - I had as a small child growing up - for all... God bless! Amen.

Shades of Gray

There at the end of another day, I entertained the thoughts of love and life that's passed me by. My life has entered its last trimester; there's no going back to vigor and youth, content with the solitude which remains; and, there staring back, the shades… where blond and brown intermingled; and, salt and pepper – well, they weren't even in the forecast. Youth has all but gone. I prop my toes upon a rail; and I watched the setting sun.

Watching the red glare through the cumulus gray; "Miraculous," I thought while sitting on the deck. "How many shades of gray are there?" Through the gray, it made a purple, a yellow, and a hint of orange; all of which I've never noticed…..the various shades that red and gray complimented in a way that only a majestic setting sun could make.

As rainbows capture the imagination; this day, as night falls –I witnessed the awesome power of custom mixed colors you couldn't paint; with soothing grace across the waters and ripples of black against the orange. "Yes, it was I that God allowed to bow to thank for the privilege to even write. As in the final scene; the red glare disappears, the earth reverently watches, and the shades of gray are all darker. Even the animals pay homage for too "they know," this movie was directed by our creator, "God." who has kissed the heavens and the earth. Somberly, the skies are in jubilation, and sparkle …even touching the faintest stars....

Now the party is over; the final scene was just for me - I guess; for I can't even begin to paint in poetry, the gift; the show, I just watched. God's grace where He's shown His light for me!!!!

Solitude

It's been four or five years; I can't remember anymore – but, it's been a long while since serenity and me, had a beach-front reunion. Driving through Dallas on thirty something at eighty miles an hour; being ran over if I went much slower, my mind found it difficult to concentrate on the solitude I was looking forward to enjoying. Being bound in the southerly direction with a group of others around me - trying not to get hit, the loneliness had set in. Realizing the difference, I was focused on my heading; and, not the path of least resistance.

So early the next morn – tired…I didn't care; solitude was out there calling my name. With nothing but a dirty pair of cut offs I wore yesterday on; I was off to where God made life; and, the earth still proclaimed its existence. No traffic jams, no yapping dogs, no screaming kids playing in the back yard; just me alone with my solitude, combing the shore, looking for keepsakes, and God - of course! The fragrance of salt dominated the air; the only noise was the roar of the ocean reflecting back to my supersonic way of life.

I wondered where'd this' been for so many years. I paused reverently to give thanks, as there before God - watching his creation; I thought, "Why Lord must we go like hell, and drive ourselves to the brink of distinction to come to your sanctuary of beauty; where solitude is so prominent, and loneliness is non-existent. For quietly, not even a whisper; the holiness of life - I turned and sat facing east, the sun about to make a grand entrance. I watched with all the shades glimmering through the rays, the colors transparent like a second coming, intensely staring! - waiting! …… a miracle!!!!

Without notice or noise, a cloud interrupted the view… or did it? The center dark, almost black, then shades of gray - and then, as God promised us all as we go through life and all its struggles ---- a silver lining prevailed. I looked and laughed to myself!
"Even a lonely ole cloud, can produce its own beauty." There I was, older now ---- laughing out loud! I guess all hope isn't over after all! Amen.

Spectacular

    Sitting in the sand, the winds picking up the salt from the sea; the spray hitting my face - I watched, and waited as the sun set behind me. The super moon was approaching. The waves looked huge as I sat on the beach, eye-to-eye with them; and, listened to the ocean roar. Nothing short of --- "Spectacular!" Watching the water; and, not paying attention...you came up behind me, leaned your knees into my back, "Hey, let's play." I turned and there looking up you stood; your skin aglow in your bloomer plaid shorts, and a sleeveless yellow sweater top; with a fluorescent green Frisbee, smiling... "Let's play catch!" I said in this wind???.... Ok!!! I'm game! Running away, I watched you as your youthfulness had miraculously returned; running in the sand in the salt air...

You cast the Frisbee at the wind over the ocean; and, then the wind returned it to me. I thought "now how cool," so I did it too. I went swimming, "How did you do that?" Now wet, I wondered... You laughed and said "come on... let's get you changed before you get too cold." "Great idea," I thought. "I need to get warm!" - The water was colder than I thought. Dripping like a drown rat passed the front desk, "What happened to you?" "Don't ask," I replied. Up to the sixth floor, I thought I might short the elevator, and all for a flipping - Frisbee.

Stripping, you started the shower for me. It felt so good! - Then the glass door opened, jumping in, you offered, "Let me wash your back." "Well, you can just imagine where this went!" Oh no, not to the bed; but, the balcony overlooking the ocean in the moonlight.... Yes, and there in the light of the night; we cuddled over the handrail. We made the most incredible discovery any two lovers could find; for there as we held on to the rail, our love - so deep; so fulfilling, it was nothing short of "spectacular!!!"

    As the heavens blessed our sanctuary of romantic holiness, the stars poised... God had created this moment as we made love under that "Super moon." It was, nothing short of "Spectacular!!!"

Stagnant

I stood beside that cattails in the early morning sun, I watched the little critters jumping around playing leap frog. And there in the warm rays, I saw a lesson; metaphorically - the stagnant waters gave light to some whose lives reminded me, "They're in a pond of life." Sadly I thought, an encompassed life of mosquito larva and cattails, lying at the perimeter; and, marshy mud at their feet, bordering life.

Engulfed in a lifestyle unsuitable to prosper, their minds and bodies lie dormant; "Stagnant" as the waters; and, the depths - shallow, held captive in the murky incoherent everyday way of life. I wonder if where they go… "Is there a life outside the pond?" And as they wander through the thing called life; stuck where believing is good enough, the weeds and cattails live; and, breathe - but leave little left for even God as they stray\ from the marsh meadows.

I think I see a ripple as the algae barely moves. I wait and watch to see if life is really sustainable there; beneath the wind swept white, painted on the crisp cool blue, as life according to God is full of vibrancy; and promise - though I've seen many ponds the thoughts of life that live within are truly, not very godly.

And today in the calm of the cattails, I turn to where love is ever present; and, joy remains a way of life as God, my lifeguard, protects me from the deep. Only He can see that life living with in a pond, gives nothing but harmony to the landscape. Thank You for the lesson, I am honored.....

Standing Alone

I locked the gate as I walked away between those marble columns; I turned around, and looked at where life for me had been prosperity, memories, and holidays which had filled my thoughts for all those many years; and baby cradles, and training wheels turning to adolescents and graduations. Where anniversaries, and caroling renewed our faith in humanity.

That was..... Until a message on the mirror had surmised it down to the value of a marriage. There where devotion and vows meant little to your cause; and, all that remained was stuff you could claim in a second hand store. I called my attorney, for all the good it would do; then the pastor - who said, "I'll pray for you." So -- in the fescue, a small benign sign read, "good home for someone who wants more out life than separation!"

Standing alone in the concrete forest, I felt the weight of every limb caving in on me. The thought of throwing away three decades of scrap books; and, photo albums of memorable moments - was more than I could bear. But I was alone - standing where life looked as a now dead-end sign hanging in front of me. God - "What had I done wrong???!!!"

The busy traffic and people out on their merry way; I watched them all, but they didn't see me...I wasn't there! My life, a memory of the day before when harmony and joy were splendid.... Walking, I found a bench in a cemetery. I sat and thought does one of those have my name inscribed on it? ... As the chill had numbed me to the bone - with tears I held back since I read your note, I balled. "God, save me!" I yelled out loud ...

My head in my hands, my elbows on my knees, staring down; was a piece of fabric. I picked it up; and. on the torn corner of the embroidery - was your initials. I looked to the clouds crying, "God, how can a gift that came before you and vowed to the end, be ripped in two.... to threads; and, all that remains is a tiny piece of your handkerchief." Watching the falling leaves, I heard your voice; "I love you" --- I thought I heard; or, was it just the wind hallowing? Then in calm - not a sound, out of nowhere...an angel came. She took my hand, "Let's walk," she said. And as we strolled, she stopped in front of a head stone that read, "good home for someone who wants more out life than separation!" I turned and asked, "What's the point?" She turned and smiled saying, "Never give up hope when your lead astray; for only God knows the road you're on!" "Blessed are you who follow".... and then; she disappeared.

"Standing alone," I knew God my comforter, was watching over me. I wasn't alone at all! But it was the hurt, the message - that grieved me so. I walked away from the cemetery, clinching your embroidered initials where there I know you cried too, for me....as well!

Standing Still

From the time we learn to walk and venture on our own to destinations unknown. We need to find the times when standing still is so beneficial. I look back to my childhood days, when I - walking down a dirt road on a lazy afternoon; came up on a little fawn There, you see her before she "scents" your presence. In the foliage, patiently you watch not understanding at a tender age that God's beauty can only be seen if we are "patiently standing still."

And there as we grow, annoyed by anything slow; as we live in a supersonic speed of hi-tech, we seem to lose the very principles of which we were raised ... for there as we grave the progress; we rush to play catch up, forgetting that "standing still" may be more productive.

Now years past, there I watch as grey covers the earth - calms waters; and, in the still morning, nature flourishes. For as a moment in time of peace and quiet, God works; and, in the evening as the red sun sets, a calming turns to still, again I remain; ever mindful… God works when we are holding on to the still as we reverently stand, watching. Rejoice!.....

Starting Over

   As I watched the seas get rougher; and, the black storm clouds roll in over us - I knew we were in for a hell of a storm. I'd rather not have to endure; the winds picked up, and pieces of shingles flew from the roof. The trees swayed as the branches didn't stand a chance.

   But there on the front porch, I watched as the lightning and thunder seemed to get worse. I knew it was over with us, before the storm even started. I stood holding onto the front porch post as you drove off! The tears were fierce as the fell like rain from the heavens to the earth; blown by the winds across my face - the sting like rain! "Hurt;" knowing there was another that had taken my place.

And then without notice, a clap so loud it was deafening. A tree snapped and split apart crashing to the ground. Like our hearts and dreams; separated by storms, we developed what came between; I screamed your name, and cried out --- But, all I saw was tail lights in the rain.

   I sat by the fire as it lit up the room all night long; I asked God, "What had I done wrong? The thunder uttered your name; and, the lightning lit up skies, as I tried to call you to come home; but, you had found a new one to rescue in the night. As the morning light came through the pane, I had fallen asleep on the couch we once shared; and, there in the simmering morning sun, you stood staring at me as I slept. I asked, "What's wrong;" and as the tears streamed down your checks you said,

"I made it to the curve - a tree split in half, and blocked the road. I couldn't go anywhere, and I fell asleep in the car in the pouring rain; and, thunder for God had stopped me before I made a terrible blunder… --- "Please…. please take me back!" "Forgive me!" "I'll never leave you again!" ……… For that; I'll promise you forever!

Super Moon

It had been an unbelievable day, a fender bender on the way to work; the boss was standing there waiting on me, as I was late. I stood there and said to God; what else can go wrong. Later that day, I was informed that all I did in the morning was backwards; traffic was horrible, and when I got home, in the candle light - dinner was on the table. There in the shimmering candlelight you sat there in your negligee, your hair was done and you were all made up. I know you could tell I'd had a horrible day. Dinner looked so good! - My favorite; fried chicken, mashed potatoes and gravy. I was so hungry that I ate two helpings. You looked at me, and said "Get a shower, I'll do the dishes."

I got a bath and tried to relax, coming out in only a robe. "Where are you, I asked, "Out on the porch, I'm watching this super moon come up over the forest." In the mysterious dark, I stood beside you. You put your hand up, and rubbed my back. I looked at you and smiled, "What are you doing?".... "Just trying to relax you, love?" I smiled and thought, she's up to no good! I said, "come…let's go to bed."

As I said good night, I rolled toward you; climbed upon you, removed the sheet; and, in the glare through the window, I kissed you as the super moon glowed on your heavenly behind. You moaned and moved as to make me stop; but, in its glare - you looked divine. I'd ever enjoyed the touch and the embrace, as you quietly enjoyed the caressing while I kissed you…. for here as heaven had touched the earth; I lay behind you, admiring what the moonlight brought to life. I rubbed and hugged your thighs; and as God gave His love to us; I fell asleep in the moonlight!.... Lying on your backside with my arms cuddling you like a pillow, you laughed as I lay, "snoring"…….

Tacking

As brutal as the winter winds – relentlessly, we weather what Mother Nature brings. We pray God has more in His offering than sub-zero temperatures that we must endure. We wait to see what another day brings, for as we go through life; we wonder, "Is this what God really want for us?" And, as the days turn to months; and, then the months turn into years - we think, "This must be our destiny"......

Never wavering, we hold on to our faith, for has not - He said, "Mine is the way," and we go believing that - what life has become, is the journey we walk; for He has lead us down this path of roses and ferns; and, daffodils and lilies - ever mindful of the stickers and thorns which lay waiting. Just as the cold and snow give way to rain and gentle winds, we must "tack" as our life changes - - - again....

As crisis brings our destinies to an end; we wait, and pray, and say, "Lord, Where are you taking me?" "Has this life I have been accustomed to been nothing more than a stepping stone that you have carried me to?" As surely as dawn will come in the morn, God's timing is His own; and, as lives have come and gone, here we are "tacking," changing our course; always going forward like sailboats on a pond, correcting - for the changing of the winds - we too must do the same.

Faith is the ability to believe that whatever life throws at us, winter winds or summer breezes, we must go on for only God sees our true destiny. If we stumble along our path; we ask our Lord, was it He that has placed the stone in our path, maybe; for God has promised life will not be easy, just keep "tacking," because the path to heaven isn't paved with gold; nor, straight into the gates of an open door. Yes, we all pray to see the light; but, it's the shadows of the stepping stones that create the curves, "tacking" - And we have no choice....

Take Me Out of the Game

   Sitting out there on the bleachers in the stars; watching the world turning, rooting for the underdog as the world beats up on the little guy! What a shame to see someone try so hard to succeed; only to get knocked down again and again. Across the pond, another world away; discontent, where human life isn't worth two cents, as there are those who have little respect for mankind; and, Christianity is a moral obligation of non-existence. Sadly, we pause in front of our TV's, and watch as killings are an everyday occurrence. And where do you think our Dear Lord is with all this going on? Turns His head maybe? I wonder! Sitting in the stars keeping score of the rights and wrongs; does it even matter anymore as we now marry our sisters and brothers with no respect to 10 commandments we can't follow. What the hell is wrong with this world?

Sitting here - meditating, alone as life has brought me to this point; I have to ask, "Why? What's the point? Where am I going?" Life has no beginning, and the end repeats itself as lightning supposedly never strikes twice in the same place. Think again! Watching as the stars move around from month to month trying to follow the northern star; a compass heading taking me in circles, trying to navigate at warp speed; I miss the turns were sovereignty has a geographic place. I'm lost out in the galaxies, waiting for a bus ride home. So I sit, and I sit, and I sit some more; waiting on a change - that seems to never come.

I hope for a brighter day, even though there are no clouds up here to block my view of things. I don't understand why in the world they are the way they are ...
But still the world turns, spinning out of control as limits are forbidden; and, the direction changes as we try follow. So we holler for help from the bottom of our desperation - for the only way is up; or so they say…. But, religiously speaking, we've been taught there's another way.

From the depths of hell to the heavens above; somewhere in the middle, is where we are struggling to maintain our mere existence. So therefore, there is no clear answer to the reasons; we are where we find ourselves positioned to climb out of the ditch we dug ourselves into. So we rest as the sun goes down; wondering what's the purpose. As God's children, we remain out in the pasture trying to find ourselves; but for me ---- I sit --- here on the bleachers, in the stars - rooting for the underdog as the game of life is almost over; and, a grand-slam in the ninth inning would only put it into extended innings............

Thank you

There as I reverently watched the sun, it's grace came with the morning warmth, for its only God, our heavenly father which delights us, as a new day of life fills our hearts while we begin our day. I watch as the dark of night slowly disappears, settling as the stars rest in the hemisphere. Out in the galaxies, heaven; home to all those who've made it there to their finally resting place; I pray and wonder.

And as the sun creeps in the morning, I give thanks as only you know my true thoughts and feelings. The love so 'bountifully' given; I'm amazed every morning as dawn brings the new. Appreciative with gratitude for the blessings You've bestowed; are truly only by the compliments from You; ever mindful, I can only thank you, and be accountable to Your honor ...Yes ...and as I venture, ever mindful of others, trying to be the best I can for only you; my strength, reaching out -Your faith in me, keeps me on my heading. I pray, "Lord be with me today and forever."

And at the end when the sun slowly settles on the horizon, and lullabies are read, I pray. I pray that the Lord protects me, as angels surround my surroundings; where my head rests in the darkness of the night. "Thank You!"

The Art of Happy Hearts

I sat and thought as doctors do; "What makes the happy heart - work in you? And – then, it occurred to me; have we missed how God, meant for it to be… is our heart connected to our smile? :) "Maybe, I should contemplate this for a while." It's possible I think, doc's got it wrong… "Why you ask?" I'll tell you why; have you ever seen a person having heart attack with a smile? So there - for you see, it's important to me, for you to be just as happy as you can be.

Then I thought, I wonder what else doc's got wrong. "Hmmm," I thought. You rub your feet to rid a headache; peroxide makes your teeth white, and WD-40, although not very sporty, takes away those aches and pains.

"Yes - maybe, I too am a Doctor Seuss of sorts!" "The remedies could change your course."

But -ah- those happy hearts!!!!! Those old folks holding hands, as they walk, does a smile come to your happy heart; for they share the same, I think; and, once I saw - two little kids….oh - 5or6. He held her hand, and ran - and ran - as fast as they can, to the other side. There was a couple little happy hearts, as they stood there on that walk, trying to catch their breath.

Of course, there are the honeymooners. "Why is she in white, and he mourns in black?" Is he full of sorrow or regret??? "No - I bet." Their happy hearts are looking forward, till the night.

So why, I wonder - must these things, lead to be confused? I read a med-journal early one mornin' while I meditated upon a stool. My happy heart was here too for me, for I was there primarily for some relief!!! The journal said, I was wrong, but the ones that wrote it are dead and gone. Were they right? I'm not sure, sitting here tonight.

So how's your happy heart doing today? Are you still smiling there - where you lay??? Maybe….or is it not? It may depend! Do you sleep in a big ole bed or is it a little cot? Rest assured, I've been in both; but, worse yet - between you and me, try sleeping on muddy ground under a canoe….No happy heart there, for it's here to there that I compare. But my happy heart, it waits for you. Does yours long for me too? Let me look "hmmmm," let's see.

So- next time you need to go to the doc's; use my philosophy! SMILE, RUB YOUR FEET, PEROXIDE YOUR TEETH; APPLY THAT NOT SO SPORTY FORTY, and call me in the MORN!!!!!

In the Blink of an Eye

Another normal day there, or so you think. The sun's rays burning away the dampness of the morning dew. The birds rejoice in the cloudless sky; people let you in for a change as you try to merge from lane to lane. The world is perfect as it continues to spin. But then the news comes, it's a stint or its terminal, and there "in the blink of eye," the world changed for you; situations and thoughts become predominant.

What once seemed so important don't mean a damn now. Priorities aren't important, somehow as life has robbed you of living 'til your ninety, is now a pipe dream of make believe.... Sadly it's just not your world that gets rocked, but friends and family; acquaintances you've barely met, and new neighbors next door. You can't explain what's happening to you - to them.

And there as the tulip tree still grows in spite of the drought, standing straight and tall all on its own; God gives it another chance at life. Humbly thanking God for a second chance, where - if it were not for our Lord, dust to dust - it would be the last. In spite of the consequences, we remain vigilant to our cause that God blesses us all.

And as we lay on our beds at night and watch the sunsets, we ask "why," yet graciously, are we? For the continuance – it's the "how come" we continue to seek..... And there in a blink of an eye our world is turned upside down, rocked by the unexpected, for it is our God that gives us the strength to journey on. As precious as life maybe, even a little tulip tree persists as we watch the moon crest!...

The Day After

In the misty cool of the early dawn, perfectly meant for coffee in bed; we sat and watched the others' smiles, so cool you could almost see your breath. But the stove radiantly gave some hope to the warmth that might be forth coming soon; and, by the second cup some peeks of blue peeked through the gray. I watched as I thought the weather was changing for the better.

Things to do - Places to go, but it only took a phone call, and plans --changed again; the stress returns and past hurts rekindle like a camp fire. There still like ambers, not a word was said. You fell asleep in the sun, as I was headed home. I watched you as your eyes were closed. Did you even see the hurt I endured? Patiently, I cared more for you than your thoughts of concern could ever be for me.

The day now clouded the weather turned, a rumble of thunder, and there the memories of past storms, reminded me of where I was not wanted. I closed the door, I walked away not looking back, for there in the autumn leaves and clouds of gray, I kissed your memory. And as the sun returned - brighter days; I look forward ... For there by God grace blessings flow, as refreshing waters of melting snows. Melt into the soul. As only God can heal the wounded spirit....

The Edge of Tranquility

I sit here at the waters' edge; and, look at life - the difference I see below and above; then, there's the other edge - the one we keep amongst our hearts, the one of which we dream; and, as I sit here at this edge of this tranquility. I wonder....could this be a message for me; I wonder if it's heaven's edge, is it not the same?

It seems to me as we are drawn to a beach somewhere; we may not like the water per se; but it's the "edge" where the two lives' meet - that is where we all seem to find tranquility. Amazingly, we are drawn!

And then - there are those who climb slopes; their challenge is the climb they face; or is it the edge between earth and space, life above - they love? They have found an "edge of tranquility," as they reach the top – it's the utopia!

There are those who walk in the woods; the path they go… they watch, and talk to things that are not, for they search their soul to find, a friend to look to; communicate within. As comfort comes; they purge themselves along the way, for they too find an edge of tranquility.

And as we go forth; we walk, and talk to those who share our side…it might be you on the right; or, might it be our father who art; and, as we love our life – tomorrow, we constantly look for today, we see tranquility "is" the edge.

As I think of those near – end; for they too have reached a place, where life and death too is an edge; and, they search for tranquility. They leave this life - they live; thoughts of things have past, the joys of those whose lives are gone…now wanting to be with those they loved.

This not an edge for here on earth, we are; and, heaven awaits - between the two; there lies tranquility, - the "edge" that God has made.

The Edge

There I stand - I hear the thunder as the heavens grumble at the edge where I am; for only God above, knows my course of direction. Not even me! Am I privy to the destination - Standing on the edge; the lightning has determined to command the sky to light the night; a storm was born in conflict; the ions battle over the murky waters; for I reach to the heavens asking God, "Why, on such a peaceful evening, must the moonlight be filled with thunder?"

And then as on command, a clap so loud…Are the heavens mad? - I believe so, for God has responded. Still, why? Why where I stand - the edge; must I feel the tears from where there once was a starry night? The heavens are crying, and there alone, my heart flutters. "Is it now my turn?" "Must I go?" "Is it my calling?"

But then without notice, the white outline against the black shadows calmed the turbulence; and on the edge, the storm has past me by. Reverently, I remain resilient to whether I remain here, for only God picks those who He wants to choose.

As the dawn of morning comes, crystals of water beads lay on lawn, serene. I think it's not my turn! Yes, God has plans for me to do His work here; being vigilant, I remain! But the warmth of the sun grows, and a refreshing breeze comes - I am blessed!

A new day dawning and promises that lay ahead - Oh Lord, forgive those who have troubled me and watch over them, for I am not their "one to keep." Yes, Lord - I give thanks to your words instilled…. I will read! - Thank you Lord for another, the compliments by your dawn…

The Garden of Eden

In the early morn as the sunlight barely appeared through the heavens, I got a glimpse of us in the "Garden of Eden." For there, as the lord pronounced; you and me, shall cultivate the earth for the heavens. As I think and measure the amount of love God gave - its' infinite number. I feel that amongst the flowers in the Garden of Eden; God has blessed me with you!

In the peace of joy, and harmony in nature; we would step out on the sandy shore, and walk the beach - frolicking to the rhythm thereof; and there as God ordered, we'd bathe in love on that shore, and lay in the romance watching the moonlight rise over the waters; and in the morning, "I" would go to pick the fruit that God had menu 'd for us to endure, and only share love; and harvest that which was safe to eat; for here in our own little "garden," - God remains as we, even now, take the sacraments of love, and cultivate - bare fruits for the future world; our children.

The love, Oh the love I have as Valentines approaches. I think of ways I could shower you with gifts to say, "I love you"... But before the roses; the thoughts of being in the Garden of Eden with you; to be the one - the only one - that God gave me to start, and create the world - how wonderful it would have been, you and me - I think...

Now, as we go through our busy day of hustle and bustle, I pray. I pray you know that of all the ones in the world - it be "you," I'd pick to join me - if God ever gave me a chance to replenish the ----" The Garden of Eden. "

The Gift-Love

I need you to sit and listen for…I need you to know – that, what you call love; may not! - God only knows what love is, does He not? In fact, does He share this with us - the gift of love - so we can share -as He?

I've been around a time or two; or, maybe more… three, or four. But, my search for love has led me to the end; where love is to adore - a good friend - guess what - it is not.

I sat one sunny afternoon, waiting on a mystery to unfold for, like a novel, the ending, I could predict, or at least I thought. So as I sit with my Sunday news, a hand comes to my shoulder; it was you! I turned and said; "How are you?" But, you might think this is the beginning to the end, or where is it going? Well my friend!!!

I never thought that love at first site was possible from behind these old eyes; and, who would know - it was 'gonna be you? Oh my!!! We met again, and cracked a beer… shelled a nut or two; we smiled, and held hands as well. "Please come home with me!" "Are you sure?" "Like never before." "What could I do; but, follow her to her palace." We went and lo-n-behold; a gift…heaven sent, for there - in my arms with all your charms; you lay. "I love you." NO you can't; it's only our second day. But I did, and there before God, I prayed that this lady I adore….. She and I would stay.

She took my hand to the promise land; "Follow me to where I lay, let us bless this love that we have found." We, long into the night, have come a very long way; and, now I know you are the one for which I prayed. "Oh," I said. "If you only knew," you're what I prayed for too; that God would bless this matrimony, the love we shared was un-compared. Who would know that it was you I met a year ago… we wasted - chasing rainbows across the fields.

So now I see the love for me was just that; but, the gift you gave; I will savor, for as we walk, hand and hand; me on the left, and you are right beside me when the day is through, and we kiss in the moon light, a candle flickers on you….the luster shows.

As the novels goes; maybe a chapter or two is all you need, you know. But, its the climax of the story - the ecstasy…… where you read in the candle light - between covers…… "You'll see!"

The Gull

In the early morn I walk to the end; and, there I sat on the bench, and watched as the fog burned off. As it lifted, it was as though my eyes were opened for the very first time; surrounded by the gray haze in the cool; and, the dew of the early morning view. The blue above poked through; and, the sea gulls flew; where the sun had warmed the air…

I watched as they fished for their morning meal. A gentle wind stirred as the fish hid in the cat paws. While sitting on the dewy dock; one decided to land, and there he and I; eye-to-eye, we met. "Good morning," I thought. He shook his head, spread his wings, and nested right there on the bench beside me. "Hmmm, do I dare move a muscle and disturb him as he's resting?"

Now focused on the gull that has accompanied me, the blue, the lifting fog, and the cat paws too; they all became a back drop to the picture that sat beside me; and as we all do in our times of tranquility; talk to God's creations as they venture too close. But this one was different! I moved a little, and there he stayed. I turned my head, and he looked my way. "This is incredible," I thought to myself. I held my hand out… surely that should do it; but, it did not.

As his friends flew above him and me, I knew they were watching too! I turned my body slightly toward him; but, still he ruffled his feathers - yet stayed right there. "Ok, I'm going to see if he'll let me pet him; surely not, but maybe so. Gently I reached with the precision of a surgeon's hand; like brush strokes, very lightly I rubbed his back. He dropped his head, and closed his eyes as to say, "Thank you for that!" I did it again; and, still he stayed.

His comfort grew, his confidence prevailed; respectfully - I petted him a time or two again; and, again - And as he let me, a bond was born and the fear was broken. As I looked to the heavens, and thanked God for this moment; me and nature were one ….for a second, I thought to myself, "Was that God reaching out to me?

"Did I meet Him as I was supposed to? – "Did I follow my conscience?" "Oh! But I did!" for no bird on this planet would land and let a hand touch him - as I did.... "Yes, I think God dropped by to pay me homage- on that cool foggy morning; just to say "Hi," and see how I was doing. I told Him I was okay by my touch, that I gave Him. And there on the bench, I watched as He took off.... He circled as to say, "Bless you, I'll see soon! --- come back again someday!!!"

The Lady in Red

There, my thoughts of deadlines and print, and the week ahead; I looked up, like the lord had spoken, and there in the choir – stood; and as I sat where so many thoughts of love; of faith and hope originate, I watched. The spirit overwhelming, like an angel - stood with a halo above her; sang from her heart. Mesmerized, I couldn't take my eyes off her.

Engulfed in my intimate thoughts of messages sent by God; now were interrupted, I sat back in my comfort zone; messages on hold. I continued to watch; for there, a group of fifty or so, harmonized in heavenly harmony, all I could do was listen. I wondered, was the lady in red a messenger, carrying a note from God for me to pay attention to her. I wonder......

But practice is over; I listen to Mary as she teaches her lesson below. I half-way listen from the balcony, but where is the lady in red – disappeared. Will she return as service starts? Was she a mirage? Did I even see her, or was I dreaming? I need to wake up ... Mary is closing; I sit in silence. I thought, you know; I laid out on my bed three different shirts, I wore red ....sharing like the blood of Jesus - an angel touched my heart! ...

The Pond

I held your hand as I help you down the hill. Heaven forbid you'd fall, or twist an ankle; but, finally managing to navigate around the piney branches loaded with snow; we found a place to sit on the park bench in the shivering cold. I put my skates on, got down on my knees to help you, and tied your laces. The frozen pond was loaded with others; I stood up and took your hand saying, "Come on! I'll help you out onto the pond; button your coat so you don't catch 'cold."

First a baby step, I watched with intent, then a push with the left and you began. I held your hand and tried to help you keep your balance. We skated around the edge until you felt comfortable to go on your own. I let you go and skated around you making lots of circles. I skated backward, took your hands in mine, and held them. I watched your eyes as they grew.

The surprised look on your face as I pulled you along, was more than any love could stand! I smiled and released you as glided along by yourself. I laughed! You yelled, "Stop laughing, I'm doing the best I can!" All I could do was keep laughing at you and then off in the middle of everyone, I etched a heart in ice for you. I called you to come see; "Look what I have done!"

You glided by; I grabbed you, and I spun you in a circle; we lost our balance, and fell to the ice where in the cold, we feel 'in love' ... And as I had etched in the ice, you carved a place into my life. Laughing, holding onto each other, a few onlookers came to help us up. Laughing at us too, we finally had found the love we were looking for....

Our Lord in the freezing cold has blessed us with His warmth; and, in our hearts we knew that with our Lord between us; we could reach the moon and even heaven wasn't far from there, as long as we had God and stayed together, skating through life......

The Road

Coming home from being on the road, I unlocked the door to my humble abode. I looked around as I put my back against the door, and closed it with my butt. Everything seemed to be just as I left it a week before; that was until I went to the bathroom; and, taped to the mirror was a note that read, "My darling, your generosity has been extravagant; your love and romance – immense; your thoughtfulness – enormous; but, the distance between our lives are miles apart; and, the doubt about your whereabouts is more than I can stand." "I know your obligations are part of your job; but, the vow we took said nothing about a life on the open road." "So my dear, I bid you a farewell, God speed, and don't you - because that damn diesel means more to you than Me!".... Good Bye!!! "

Standing there - alone in the restroom with all I had left from you… a "Go to hell love letter," that you wrote. I looked in the mirror and asked God, "What do I do?" Staring there, deep within the nickeled glass, the mirror shattered into a million pieces. Some fell in the sink, some on the floor. I jumped back and yelled - "Oh my God!"

And from out of the cracks in the glass, Satan smiled - "It's me again!" – "I've come to ruin your life once more!" "How am I doing?" To you devil I said, "You've wrecked my home, and destroyed my life!" Where's my wife?" "You did this to her - didn't you?" - You bastard! - I said…. as I turned and walked away. I flipped the switch to off, and said "Go away!" As I left the mess where it lay, I walked into the kitchen, stood over the stove and prayed, "Lord what's going on here, did I deserve this?

And as I stood there with my eyes closed, God spoke -

" My son --- my son, I love you - and what you have done was not keep Me between you and your loved one - allowing Satan to part take in your intimacy." I watched as you drove cross country and forgot the vow you made - you so often broke,"

So here now alone, a broken hearted mirror reflecting the shattered pieces of the love letter clinched in my left hand. He continued, "You brought shame where there was honor and love - that I bought - So now, I beseech thee, go find thy love you gave birth to - hold her in your arms - and remind her that it is "I " your God, that controls your destiny - now "GO" go in Peace !! "

The Score

Today in the rain, I walked away from the grave; from a relentless friend who stood by my side. He was there for me when the sun was warm, and there too when the times were not so bad. Yet he too showed in the middle of the night, and stood, stared at me by my bed side. In the morning as I woke sometimes; no matter how hard I prayed -"he'd" remain there with me.

The dirt hadn't settled before I knew the friend I buried had a twin brother who decided to move in, as his other had given up the ghost and died off to another world... But in the night, restless and weary; I tossed and cried, as my pillow did little to comfort. Still I lay there, and thought of you wondering why would - you do that – it's terrible! I thought, to be caught up in two lives lost, for I could see where I wanted to be lying naked, alone with another?

And in the middle of the night at my weakest point; my conscience again had denied me the right of another night's sleep. I worry and try to justify things that are; and, wake …turn, and look at the other pillow – "Why?"

Day and night, I try to put the twins behind, and out of my mind; but, they persist…following me like a shadow. I can't seem to shake them from my life; but it seems it's only in the serene - I get a minute of peace where the twins don't bother me. And even though there's a spiritual connection between the two, "the good and the evil," as my conscious mind battles over who is wrong, and who is right!

As Gods sits on the sidelines watching - like a ping pong tournament, we try to pray for the game to end, but it continues. Today, in prayer and faith; I look for peace, and joy - waiting to see who serves next. Yes, I see God in the bleachers as he turns his head back and forth - looking at the board…. the score is nothing to nothing --- Nobody wins!.....

The Wall

"You need to see what I see," I said. "It's a wall I feel, that has become 3D –right there in front of me!" Then I wondered, "Why are there so many walls in the world - from relationships, to the China Sea; the walls are vast and ominous from the way we live our lives to every breath we breathe.

"So why are walls all around us?" "Why do walls become so visible;" Why are they so indescribable?" I met someone once that lived behind a wall. I asked them, "Who are you?" "Do you even know?" Sadly, they sat and stared at the wall looking through it for me, and agreed...They couldn't see me either, for this obscure structure had buried them, and made their life a mockery. How sad I thought! God never made a wall; but, we are carpenters - with hammers, and saws.

"Are walls just there to keep us in; or, - us - out; or, are they there to turn us about, and doubt?" For I love my immeasurable space...no boundaries. "Are you happy or content, being held captive in the confines of your own mind? Are you the Ruler of your space or some great land - that encompasses from sea to sea; or, is it just a barrier you put up to protect yourself from me?

Walls for centuries have controlled and limited; not those that are out, but those within; for the walls you build only hurt you; your heart; your mind; your spirit, too. I ask myself, "How would Our Lord handle this? "Would He agree? - Probably not!!!" Behind your wall, I wonder, "Have you shut out the love you hunger, the one you adore?" "How do you breathe, strapped to a wall that's holding you bound, to the sound of your disharmony?" My heart hurts as God and me, try to break through the elusive wall created by your history.

"I am sorry....my love's not that strong to help you remove the wall that imprisons you." Not even God can give you the strength to remove that shield - you call "a wall." So sadly I see - the wall that encompasses your heart, as it too - is broken; suspended in the vacuum of the void of life, you try to ignore.

The Wilted Flower

I thought, "If they were in the sun, they'd thrive and live a lot longer." But the water was too warm sitting there - so I moved the bouquet to the center of my hand rubbed drop leaf table where they would be admired, proudly congregating in the vase in my dining room.

The Vase filled with jonquils, tulips, baby's breath and ferns; and, lilacs and lilies too; but also protected from view, a Lady Pamela Carol with all her distinct beauty and character, stood amongst the other flowers trying to mingle, yet with such grace - noticeably she took her place by herself. With solitude and effervescence, Lady Pamela Carol, though not tall - stood alone capturing what life had to offer.

A million dollar bouquet that could just light up a room by itself – our Lady Pamela with all her fragrance, quietly poised amidst the flowers....

One day, I noticed on my table, one of my flowers was wilting away, hurriedly I rushed to remove the others to let my wilted one get a breath; but, there before me as I held her in my hands, my wilted flower, Lady Pamela - faded. The rest knew they lost one of their own, as they all drooped reverently to honor her.

I lay my little flower on a white linen and said a prayer; "Lord, before you lays a lady of eloquence, a flower Lord, Lady Pamela Carol, my little rose, take her dear Lord; give her life in a meadow in heaven; and, as you stand guard Lord, may Lady Pamela be by your feet, lining the pathway to heaven for others to follow " ...Amen!

Thoughts!!!

In the middle of the bed, I laid my head, praying; and, as I did - interrupted by a voice that's answering the prayer as though the call – intentional, for it's true that all things are due to Gods timing. And in the middle of her bed, she lays her head; upon her pillows – gasping; with thoughts of love, and answered prayers - are in the power of her hand, as she picks up the phone to call.

A benign conversation begins, "Hi…Were you sleeping?" And as the night grows so does thoughts of anticipation; for in the dark, a spark ignites, and the questions, stories that recollect; are passed, shared; we give attention to the responses. Similarities are found as dialog continues, and utter chatter turns to "deep in thought," for there as our pillow conversation warms, a sense of respect - preludes love which grows as we share our pillow talk together.

And as morning breaks, in the middle of the pillows you wake; and, the first thoughts of your morning ritual are interrupted as morning coffee and conversation begin once more. "Ah! – the Romance!" How we cherish the thoughts … here our hearts mingle like making breakfast together on Saturday morn; such a lovely thought to share - laying here alone, thinking of you; as you lay at home in your bed…thinking of me as well!---

Today

    I woke this morning and sitting on the edge of the bed; I was in such despair! So many things I'd worried about seemed stuck, right in my head. I even called my trusted friend. His advice you know, would surely help; but, he was at a loss for things that could cure, and put things on the mend.

    As if that wasn't bad enough, a call came that I never expected. My heart sank with the impending news. My body crushed beyond my wildest dreams! I sat on this broken bench knowing just how it felt.

    I sat on that bench with all of this despair. A light from heaven appeared to me; it shined so brightly in my eyes. Here before me, an angel stood - much to my surprise! O' Lord have you heard my dreams? The angel smiled and said, "Yes, we heard your screams." She remained with me all afternoon. We spoke and laughed till the sun set. I asked, "What can I do to repay this debt?" Again she smiled, and looked at me saying, "I came because of you, for it was you that needed me." Even angels need love too! I wanted to have that love from you.

    I said, "Mam;" not knowing how to address her. "Mam, I'm at a loss for words!" She started to drift away. I said to her, "You made my day," and as she faintly disappeared - you know… I think I heard her say, "You're such a dear! I will be right here for you too."

Touch

Yes, there are those who go through life from birth to adolescence; from puberty to marriage; husbands and wives going through our daily day of responsibilities; and, find success in stuff that has "no substance." Love as it comes and goes through our legacies of life; we seem to ignore what is the nucleus of God's gift; for God gave us a gift…but, this gift goes much further than giving…it's the "Touch."

The word alone, "touch," - a verb or a noun, for it has come to be a word – renown; and, as in nurturing life in the infancy stages of creation…life starts with a touch; and, as we love life, and try to navigate from beginning to end, touch has been the little thing - that keeps us coming back….again and again.

For me - I see the touch I miss so much, is where love, "the gift" - comes from touch. I listen to a friend that states - nothing means more to them than the touch. And now I see that love…as great as it may be, is a gift from above. Touch is where love starts; a gift that God has allowed us to share.

From fabric to food, from feathers to flowers; from a baby's skin; to spending hours - with the one who made the gift of love; from there within, "touch" is where all things stem.

As she explained, life is nothing without a brief encounter of caring. I thought, "How basic is the thought of sharing? "Oh, I wonder how many come and go never knowing - the value of the touch. We talk about relationships and companionships when we get old - but it's the touch that demands of us - to step out in the cold and give the gift - that God above - by design - gave to us all.

Yes I see where you maybe; not lost for love, but hunting for the touch - the nucleus of all, the thoughts that are derived from above.

God has brought us a lot - to have upon this earth- from birth - we search for love - a special gift that comes in - the form of love – "Touch!"

Trust

In my right hand pants pocket; a pocket full of change – and, "they" all in fact, say the same thing; and, as tomorrow brings another - new for us to live we pray too; "Our father… we trust in you, and the life we believe in; may be blessed by you; our king ... But as we believe in love, and it is to be coupled with "trust, we find it hard, as so many of us carry on; living in their own private lives .... I watched where love was exposed but trust was ignored......

And there at your feet, the family dog lays waiting for your command; a love and respect, where you trust - well okay, trust he won't bite you! - Maybe. A men's best friend -- I wonder why it's not your better half? An entertaining thought to say the least, I don't understand… you mean you'd trust a dog over a human? One thing's for sure… a dog's trust will never falter.

Muted in life where it's believed – its better, not to tell everything you know - allowing doubt to grow inside your heart; and, love bridges the gap, where trust and respect have lost their prospective position. – It's there when you feel the change. Does faith enter in? Should we have trust in thee, or should it be "in God, let faith reign!"

Me, I believe that respect and trust equals love; and as I do go and pray, it's my faith that builds trust while it lies sleeping. Waiting on the same, my best friend, not four legged - but one who hugs you around the waist; brings you coffee in the morning; and, not one that runs out for the morning paper.

The one who you can share grace with and God is part of everything that lives …… between you ………..Amen!

Turn the Page

The summers' heat in those oppressive days; a cool snap, breaks the wave. We step outside - to take a deep breath; and, smile as we feel the diminished heat. Winter's grip has held us captive to the cold - our bodies frozen, with nowhere to go to get warm; holding our feet to the fire as the heat rises up the flue. Spring will be a welcome relief after the last freeze lying on the lawn.

Time - a thermo in life where we too must change. I see, as things repeat that there is a calm where we to pause to rest; and as on a job as life tries to catch up in that space of nothingness; God asks us to wait, and be patient. For "He," working over time for us, trying to grant us our sovereignty…the love for life, as it replenishes our souls in our hearts; we reverently respect.

There in the early morn, a comfort comes to you as though God has waved His magic wand and blessed you for a new life has been born again. Our hearts are warmed in the It won't be long before its spring…right now, its 3 degrees. The comfort of cold - kills the germs that crawled in us and soiled our souls; for our hearts deserve better! - We turn the page, and realize our lives have sadly lost their fragrance of happiness and joy, we once called love.

And as the bible spoke of widows' walk; we all are victims of death, where love is lost. I look, "Where is that brighter day of which they talk?" – "On its way? I turn the page for God said we deserve that which He promised! - I gave as I was taught, I shall not stop! Haunted by the past, we all have widowed thoughts of paths where we once walked.

So dear Lord, I pray today is the day you - turn the page for me; and, save me from my fears where I have walked – which have disappeared from my memories ……of spirit.

Warm Thoughts

    Sitting here watching as winter comes, broker than a settin' hen; waiting on the things Spring brings; the first frost will soon be here. The leaves now browned, and most of them have fallen, whirling around upon the ground. Thoughts of family come to mind, a time for giving to the ones, I love.

    There's not much left of my family, but my brother and me, staying in touch is a must, especially at Thanksgiving. I thought of days I'd like to share of others with; but all I see is my brother and me, as falling rain changes to snow.

    And as the winter gray, and cold lay dormant in my heart, the bitterness is so surreal; winter winds tug upon my soul. The lack of work escapes me, my budget straps my whereabouts; yet still I dream of setting suns, somewhere in the south, where waters' still kissed by the tropic sun and flowers bloom along the shore. "Oh, I wish - I was there, once more.

    So, I guess this is it! What it's come down to, about eight hundred square feet. …Can't get lost in a driven snow from the street to my front door. The birds have left their mark; footprints in the snow, but they too will soon be gone, in the mornin' sun that glows. But today is cold and gray, a flurry in the air; but, as I sit and think "it's one day closer to that "Spring." "I love you brother!"

Watching You

    I sat swinging on the front porch watching you as you knelt amongst the roses, and the crepe myrtle; a portrait framed in my mind as you sat and pruned away the dead in your flowery dress, and a pretty apricot sweeter. You looked like angel in the foliage.

    From afar – once, I watched as you congregated with friends from church, as they were enticed with what you had to say….Mesmerized as you conversed. I loved to stare across the room, proud of you as you told a story of interest they listened to you.

    And then one night I watched as things somehow just didn't seem quite right. Not sure when or what had happened – "Was it me? – "Did I say something you didn't like?".... I thought and wondered as I notice your hugs had gotten weaker; and your phone stood silent and out of sight. Something wasn't right.

    I went to church by myself for the first time since we married. The pastor stopped me after service, asking me if you were under the weather. I paused as the response needed to be polite. I didn't have the heart to tell him what I thought.

    But there somewhere - feelings had changed course; and, what was - is not any more. In the early dawn, I watched you. The tenderness that held us close, now drifted as a boat on an outgoing tide. Was there no recourse? – For only our Lord controls our conscience. We pray and ask dear God to save; but, then deep down in --- we know --- it's our passion that makes us all a slave to which drives our ego! ....

Water's Edge

    It's an unusual cool day for June; the clouds have made an awesome blanket to shade us from the oppressive heat. I spent the afternoon straightening up from the past week. Watching the rain and listening to thunder as it drowns out the dryer. I had my honey-do-list of things that I needed to do for me. I caught myself in a little déjà-vu thinking about my mom and dad; I sat and looked at the pictures I took outside their home where I grew up on the Severn.

Catching crabs with my best friend, Kirk; we'd bring home a bushel basket just from off the pier; and, the poles where it stood. Our parents loved us!!! Those were the days! .... But that was half a century ago when we were young and found ways to entertain ourselves besides watching Howdy Doody! ....

Yes I looked at the old pier as it stands majestically over the water; where serenity comes to mind as those peaceful memories remain. The stories this pier could tell and the history it could share; I - amazingly held captive at the water's edge. And, it's here that God blessed the love where my childhood remains for I am blessed to look back a half a century ago; and, nothing has changed – it's just as I left it!

    Now as my years are mostly over, I return -- in thought – it's to share my new love with the memories of my roots. Oh Lord, the love I have - the heritage I have to share with her --- incomparable; a history book by itself; recollections of events of many, many years to pass on to the children.

    But most of all, its mom and dad --- as I pray for them - as they sit with you. I could never show the appreciation that's lead me back to where my little life started, and today I want to share what God has done, allowed me to be part of. I love you more than you ever know; for I bring gifts as God would request of us all; to share the love, and the harmony of life to all... God bless! ....Amen!

We

Its 4:30, I can't sleep; disturbed by my thoughts, and memories of you. I tossed and turned trying to get you off my mind - but as I pray to God to release me from those thoughts, He draws me closer... I'm really not sure if you feel what I see, for as the lord works in mysterious ways ... We think, "we" need to move on, and go our separate ways; but, confined where memories and love for one another; we pray for guidance; but still, imprisoned - our minds are held captive to that tenderness, and joy that only comes - once in a lifetime!

I reach out to you through Jesus Our Lord; through my faith in God, you will return... I pray, the angels will do their work! Surround you as you wonder off, looking for an illusion of sorts; I can only watch my heart mourn, for our love will never be matched. I try to find the comfort that's gone as an open window. It's been released out in the cold and snow; now our hearts are frozen in time. Moving on, "is" only an illusion; we can't let go.

Now a new day of opportunity arises, where peace is a place in your soul. Regrettably, memories remain in control. Angels remind us of the love we grew fond of; the comforts of our newly established ways, those irreplaceable acts of kindness we shared. So as I welcome you to focus on those other avenues; right or wrong - the hills and pastures, and tall tree lawns... they captivate your mind as you travel on; but, I beseech thee to remember the paths, and the gardens where we walked along together. For all the roads in the world they too --- are dead end streets!
Amen....

What If

So God, "What- if!" - - - What if we never had a cross word, or never knew how to hate, or war around the world. What if trust was all we had, would that be so bad? What if? What if love was all we had, and ever knew; what if fear - forever present, was not; for love controlled our lives, and hate was non-existent! What if respect was premier, and for the love of God; respect would lead us through our lives, and the honor - divulged unto husbands and wives.

What if children lived in joy for childhood was nothing more than laughter, comfort with no remorse? - What if our tone in our voice, were never course; or, our tongues spoke no lies; our eyes shown through with the love of life, as frowns were always smiles. What if holding hands was the only sign language; that only showed we love, we embraced, nothing more! - Not control - nor frustration. What if death was rejoicing as we looked upon our loss, as a promotion to those who graduate from Earth?

What if – God; we lived by faith; love showed no fear, for happiness through generations created memories of legacies we could trace. What if sadness, or strife, or poverty were wealth, lavish and joy? What if - our hearts were full of Christmas cheer; we share with those we met, and would last throughout the year. What if "I do" meant till the end, not till someone new; or "I love you" meant only you; and no one else would ever do! ----

And then I asked; what if God never gave his son for us; or second chances - which even Jesus was denied. What if God - didn't love - what if we were deprived?

So as I close my thought, "What if!"- What if I never wrote; what if you never read what if? What if we never met; would there be a love; would there be happiness? - Oh maybe?

But because we met, and God is God; and Jesus is his only son; and, we are allowed a second chance for which we were promised; we will never live in - "What if!"

Where Angels Tread

As the dew gives way to the mornin' sun; and, as it glistens across the lawn; I wonder have we ever met the angels that surround us as we lay asleep, and then are gone in the early dawn? And, as I sit and ponder; are angels old and numbered; or might there be some new ones that God has commissioned to protect His chosen ones?

We read about the angels that are spoken of biblically. Are they dead? Are they gone? Do they not live on? And as I sat, and I caught a glimpse of footprints left in my lawn, they seemed to walk away from here; before the early dawn. "Hmmmmm," I thought, an intruder I suppose; or maybe not! Was I one of God's chosen ones?

Do angels tread among us as we go through our daily lives; and, are they here protecting me by their grace, keeping me alive? So many questions I ask God as He listens - as I write. The answers' clear angels are here; and, every now and then - they too are known to roam, and walk around; checkin' in on those chosen ones.

Yes, I have met one in Wal-Mart of all places; and know of another too! One was my closest friend, who God had taken to help Him; and friends of mine have spoken of the very same. Yes it's true! We are here, "Where Angels Tread."

Be blessed as God has paved a way. His mercies are forever more; whether we are awake, or asleep in bed; we are surrounded, "Where Angels Tread!"

Where Are You

Today it's a morning spring; a commemorative day of the second coming. I paused on a park bench, watched and thought. I looked at the paths that wander through the woods. Where dear and squirrels scammer through, above my head; a nest of little ones waiting on their morning bread.

I thought, "God, I am here: are you not; and, as I look from within; he brought - "life," all around me, breathing and thriving. He is close; but I am alone, for its only "You" I talk to. I wait, I pray; "Where are you?" I sit quietly, a little spotted fawn - Inquisitive, and pokes his nose from behind a tree I watch! Can you see there is love; as we share a moment in time together, brief as it may be! We look at what we are trying to understand, patiently I wait, I pray. "Where are you?"

For it's in the morn where we are replenished by The Lord; who gives us His grace, and we look at the paths; we make choices like the wild life that frolic in the woods… I search for you! Gently, a breeze moves the stems of the ole ferns. The stillness, serene; but yet, I find a comfort. Yes, God has blessed me! I long, I wait, I pray; "Where are you?"

Today I pray! I pray our paths may become one; where God and love, build a freeway through our hearts. We, yoked in greatest gift, God could give; for it's only the joy that comes from above, we share in thought. I wait; I pray! "Where are you? ……."

Where

    As the sun shines through the window, Carol King plays in the back ground; watching the leaves as the pass by my window. I realize today how a leaf must feel as it falls away to the ground after being released from what had kept it alive for so many months. The winter winds blow; and, the little leaf spirals out of control. The beautiful blue sky reminds me though; there's a life above if we can only find out how to get there. But why; why must we wait to see God's gift of eternity as we suffer here on earth?

    As the sun shines of promise and warmth; and, the snow gives way to the running streams that ramble through the woods. I wonder where it goes as my love too, has wandered off on a journey that leads our paths to cross; even if it was for only a brief moment in time. My heart now feels like it was drug through a grave yard; where other loves now lie below - broken too; where hurts endured from rocky roads. I think I should be happier now that it's over; but, I'm not still sitting in the window, wondering will you ever return; maybe someday… I'll never know.

    And as the warmth penetrates the pain, my heart still cold from the night before; where love kept me warm - but all that remains is the simmering ambers, glowing in the dark. My God has maybe changed His mind; or, has He just set a stumbling stone in the walk way of time as my life has had to tack from the course I was on. My sails ruffle in the chilling winds as I must start over again.

    Oh God, "Why today" have you left me here alone; separated from love that kept me warm; that you created in me, and gave – then took away. "Why?" - Maybe I loved too much; or maybe you saved me! I look back where this disaster took place and I now realize to stay would have only caused more grief to me ---my heart was already broken!

Where Life Ends

There in the lifeless desert, tumble weeds whisper as the winds howl across the drifts; and, ripples in the sand – a shed skin; where life ends and life begins anew. Rocks of stone millions of years old, entombed in a lifeless surroundings, resurrected when God created the earth; and, mountains erupted as gases deep beneath exploded; but here - life looms, and buzzards soar hundreds of feet above the ground, as creatures crawl; and, the food chain is satisfied, 'life ends' in the dark of night.

And as morning breaks, little creatures crawl out of the protective sand that blankets them like a cocoon. The sun warms, and life starts over again. As if Mother Nature has her way, as all God's creatures share in the chain as life goes on.....

But then there's another - where faith, and belief enter in; and, God has chosen - yes, we must go on believing in our own human dignity. There in the morning, getting up is a little slower…now older; things instinctively become more precious. Watching the flowers as they regain their strength; and, little birds fight to see who going to get the seed.

The little things once taken for granted, matter more than ever. And, as we find ourselves in a time capsule, embodying ourselves - we live out our dreams, praying God allows us another day.

As prayers are repeated, and only by faith do we live; life goes on - never knowing what God has in store for us. We must not give up, no matter what the adversities. I pray - I pray to God for all of my beloved friends, prosperity and happiness in our pursuit of what God has in store for us all. Amen!....

Wye Oak

It was in the autumn leaves we played, and buried each other under those massive branches of that old Wye Oak Tree; you in your pretty white lacy dress; and, me in my 501 jeans. We had it made, a future full of dreams. We knew, like winter - it was going to be tough at times; and, we knew if there was going to be a prayer - that God himself would tie the knot for a love so rare - no one could believe that of which we shared; but, under that Wye Oak tree, we played in the leaves; and, kissed, hugged, and promised our dreams; and, between the protruding roots - " I kissed your heart " for the love I found, had finally found me too.

Winter was rough, and that old oak shivered in the cold and stripped of its dignity, left there to suffer Mother Nature's brutality. We snuggled under the covers, and watched it snow. I even brought you coffee, it was much too cold to get out of bed. The roads were impassable, and in the dead of cold --- "I kissed you heart once more, and - kept it warm."

Spring brought promise as the March winds howled over the barren branches of that old oak; but, there in the depths of faith and hope - I kissed your heart once more. Oh the fragrance like an orchard as the peaches ripened; and, kissed by the sun. Romance was breath taking, for a love no one could have known was captured there; and you, in that spring, I kissed your heart. You - you knew you meant everything to me; but then one cold and dreary day, I went back to where we join our hearts and played.

The old Wye Oak had lost its new spring leaves; and, the branches sagged in the wind, withering. I looked where I kissed your heart a long time ago; and, there on the bark - a piece of lace still stuck to the tree where we fell in love. I called out your name; but, you were gone; and then in the dreary drizzle; I called again, an echo permeated the branches above; but, still the love that once was - now had washed by the rain; the love was over, the pain remained; and, there under what once was, I kissed your heart again; but, this time was good bye for the love I knew was shared; and, though I thought was only mine, I walked away, and cried for I like the old Wye Oak Tree - standing tall and strong; could only take the elements so long; and, then I too.....

Yard Sale

The day after, my best friend came over to see if they could help. Bewildered and helpless, not knowing where to start; we sat there on the edge of the bed holding each other, sobbing - remembering all the good times we had. This was going to be very hard, as everything around me reminded me of him. At a time when the whole world seems like its collapsing, I had no idea what I was going to do with all the things that meant so much to us. All those memories, the keepsakes of places we shared; Christmas and birthday gifts, cards that didn't mean much anymore.

Friday came, and in the pouring rain; I knelt in the mud and kissed your casket, "good bye for good." There in pain, I left you for the last time. Trembling, wondering as the rest of what's been normal now changed; not knowing where to start, the limousine ride gave little relief - soaking wet! I needed to change and get out of these wet things.

By the end of the next week after sorting and boxing, early on a Saturday - I walked to the edge of the drive; and, stuck a sign in the ground which read, "Yard Sale!" Yes, all our many years of matrimony, a week later had turned into a yard sale. Sadly, the value on the memories was priceless, though the little tags said fifty cents, and all items in the box were a quarter. The next day I went to church. I thought - I'd sinned, selling your stuff; but, as I was comforted by the congregation singing, there was somehow a peace in His presence.

I went back to your grave, reverently praying. I thought about how much I'm going to miss you; and, for what it's worth, I grossed three hundred, fifty seven dollars and sixty-seven cents - not very much for all the love we had shared together.
And now on our anniversary, I went out to dinner to commemorate your life with kids. There will never be another you! With sadness, I look back at all our many years of love only now resolved - to not much more than a "Yard Sale!"

You

    I lay there beside your warmth, where love like an engine, has generated so much power; steam was spilling over. As I quietly watched you sleep, you reached for me to touch, and comfort you during your dream. I dare not move to avoid disturbing you as you lay- so at peace; would only resemble - a sin. Then, to watch you sleep, and breathe so deeply, was heavenly. I watched as a little grin came upon your face. I started to laugh, wondering what was you were thinking. I couldn't destroy the moment…sleeping like a baby - you moan; and now - I'm trying to put two and two together. I was so curious as to what you were dreaming about.

    But, now I too, mesmerized by you - stuck under the linens where love and warmth from night before linger; between my thoughts, and your dreams. The love we share captivates and controls our every thought. I can tell as I watch your face… a smile, seemingly; happiness has found its way into your heart.

To think about getting up to bring you a cup of coffee, I'd ruin what I'm enjoying while watching you smile as you lay dreaming. This is true love! Knowing you're so sound asleep, and grinning from ear to ear. "Oh God, I never knew that the words - I love you - could be only spoken; here before the dawn under the covers, dreaming of loving me over again by a mere smile; and, that you don't even know, I'm seeing….. ;). I love you, which you don't even know what I'm seeing!

Table of Contents

By God's Grace-Edgewater

Written by Dana S. Bicks

1. 12 Degrees
2. A Blessing From Above
3. A Day to Remember (9/11)
4. A Night With You
5. A Quarter Moon
6. Am I – I Am
7. Autumn Shadows
8. Behind the Blind
9. Breaking Bread
10. Breathless
11. Bus Ride
12. Castles in the Sand
13. Charred Remains
14. Chasing Rainbows
15. Christmas List
16. Closing Doors
17. Cuddling on the Couch
18. Dancing with You
19. Dearly
20. Dreaming of You

21. Dreams
22. Driving Through Heaven
23. Eye of the Needle
24. Eyes of An Old Man
25. Finish Line
26. Fish Bowl
27. Footprints
28. Fortunately
29. Gifts
30. God's Art
31. God's Stage
32. God's Timing
33. God's Vestibule
34. God's Watching
35. Gone Fishing
36. Goodbye
37. Grains of Sand
38. Grandma's Rocker
39. Here
40. Here's Where I Am
41. Hey God…Ya Got a Sec
42. Him, He, Mom & Me
43. Homage
44. Honest To God
45. Horizons

46. If Time Stood Still
47. Illusions
48. In the Blink of an Eye
49. In Tune
50. Inspiration
51. Islands
52. It's a Pretty Day To Walk in the Shade
53. Jessie's Dad
54. Last Dance
55. Life
56. Mallards & Monkeys
57. Marooned
58. Maybe Later
59. Melting
60. Memories
61. Missions
62. More Wax
63. Morning
64. Mothers
65. My Carol
66. My Christmas List
67. My Last Day
68. My Walk
69. Nature's Dignity
70. Never Enough

71. Never Knew
72. No Regrets
73. Our Crowns
74. Peace
75. Pillow Talk
76. Rainy Day Decisions
77. Recollect
78. Second Thoughts
79. Senseless
80. Serenity
81. Shades of Gray
82. Solitude
83. Spectacular
84. Stagnant
85. Standing Alone
86. Standing Still
87. Starting Over
88. Super Moon
89. Tacking
90. Take Me Out of the Game
91. Thank You
92. The Art of Happy Hearts
93. The Blink of an Eye
94. The Day After
95. The Edge

96. The Edge of Tranquility
97. The Garden
98. The Garden of Eden

99. The Gift – Love
100. The Gull
101. The Lady in Red
102. The Pond
103. The Road
104. The Score
105. The Wall
106. The Wilted Flower
107. Thoughts
108. Today
109. Touch
110. Trust
111. Turn the Page
112. Warm Thoughts
113. Watching You

114. Water's Edge
115. We
116. What If
117. Where
118. Where Angels Tread
119. Where Are You
120. Where Life Ends
121. Wye Oak
122. Yard Sale
123. You

Made in the USA
Charleston, SC
22 December 2014